On This Journey We
Call Our Life

Marie-Louise von Franz, Honorary Patron

**Studies in Jungian Psychology
by Jungian Analysts**

Daryl Sharp, General Editor

On This Journey We Call Our Life

Living the Questions

JAMES HOLLIS

To Jill, to our children, Taryn and Timothy, Jonah and Seah, and to the people of the C.G. Jung Educational Center of Houston. I also thank Daryl Sharp for his vision, and for sharing the gift of analytic psychology with so many others.

Canadian Cataloguing in Publication Data

James Hollis, 1940-
   On this journey we call our life: living the questions / James Hollis

(Studies in Jungian psychology by Jungian analysts; 103)

Includes bibliographical references and index.

ISBN 1-894574-04-4

1. Self-perception.
2. Individuation (Psychology).
3. Jungian psychology.
I. Title. II. Series.

697.5.S43H64 2003   155.2   C2002-901464-6

INNER CITY BOOKS
Box 1271, Station Q, Toronto, ON M4T 2P4, Canada

Telephone (416) 927-0355 / FAX (416) 924-1814
Web site: www.innercitybooks.net / E-mail: sales@innercitybooks.net

Honorary Patron: Marie-Louise von Franz.
Publisher and General Editor: Daryl Sharp.
Senior Editor: Victoria Cowan.

INNER CITY BOOKS was founded in 1980 to promote the understanding and practical application of the work of C.G. Jung.

Cover:"Life as Ring," mixed media on canvas; Zhou Brothers, Chicago.

Printed and bound in Canada by University of Toronto Press Incorporated

CONTENTS

See final pages for descriptions of other Inner City Books

Acknowledgments

Publisher's Foreword

James Hollis writes from the heart. He also writes out of his own experience. In addition, in spite of the impressive well of learning embodied in his various books, he is just as befuddled as the rest of us when it comes to knowing the "right" way to live—and he admits it.

To my mind, Hollis's humility distinguishes him from the many others who crisscross the globe these days imparting their words of wisdom. Their learned wisdom may be right for them, but is it right for us? Does it accord with our experience? Such questions are seldom raised, stilled by the hope of imminent transformation through a group experience.

James Hollis pits us against ourselves. He delivers wisdom in spite of his doubts. His attitude is supremely Socratic. He is more interested in motivating us to question ourselves than in giving us answers. He is more interested in fruit than flowers, in wheat than chaff, in substance than fluff.

A comment by Jung comes to mind:

> The *opus* consists of three parts: insight, endurance and action. Psychology is needed only in the first part, but in the second and third parts moral strength plays the predominant role.[1]

Hollis assumes some psychological insight in those who read his books. But he does not assume we have the moral strength to endure our conflicts, our struggles with relationships, our multitudinous fears, nor does he assume that we are morally strong enough to act on our insights. He does, however, identify what trips us up, what stands in the way of being ourselves, of having an authentic life.

The ten questions/chapters in this book concern issues that

---

[1] *Letters*, vol. 1, p. 375.

bedevil us all. We can dismiss them, and we habitually do, for we all have busy lives dealing with outer matters. However, I think readers will find that it is not so easy to forget them. They will haunt you, stick to you like crazy glue, which, they say, holds some airplane parts together, so perhaps they will do the same for us.

We all fail miserably at being our best. James Hollis knows this about us, but judges not for he knows it about himself too. That is why we love him.

Daryl Sharp

The meaning of my existence is that life has
addressed a question to me . . .
or, conversely, I myself am a question."
—C. G. Jung. *Memories, Dreams, Reflections.*

Introduction
Walking in Shoes Too Small

We are lived by powers we pretend to understand:
They arrange our loves; it is they who direct at the end
The enemy bullet, the sickness, or even our hand.
—W.H. Auden.

I am among those who believe that C.G. Jung has not yet been discovered, or at least sufficiently appreciated, even over these several decades since his death in 1961. As a person, he was a man of many flaws, as we all are. As a great man, his shortcomings were also great. Where he was unconscious, he hurt himself and others, as we all do.

Confusing this all-too-human person with his contribution to our self-understanding is like saying, as a colleague once expressed it, that, since Einstein had an extramarital affair, we should now look askance at the theory of relativity. Jung was sometimes vain, self-aggrandizing and exploitative of others, but who among us has never been so?

As a visionary who reflected on the landscape of modernism, and who charted the spiritual/psychological relocation of meaning from sacred institutions to the individual, Jung was unparalleled. While none of us should turn to Jung to direct our lives, or grant him authority over our personal experience, no one offers greater insight toward a more conscious conduct of this journey we call our life. Yet, toward the end of his life, he confessed that he felt as if he had failed in his life mission.

That mission had been to convince people that a broad spirituality courses within each of us, that it is possible to find a new depth of relationship to one's faith tradition if desired. He also held that those who no longer feel at home in any institutional confession, can also gain access to the life of the spirit through a

11

personal encounter with the spontaneously generated symbols which rise from the soul. Those symbolic incarnations, he believed, link us directly to the great energies which drive the universe, and which seek their purposes through the individuation project which each of us embodies.

It dismays me to realize that even many who are training to become Jungian analysts have not read and reread Jung, preferring other writers in analytical psychology or other psychological metaphors and traditions. As valuable as those metaphors and traditions may be as additions, I believe Jung's own *oeuvre* needs to be returned to over and over and over.

In my own analysis in Zurich, my analyst would frequently ask me, "And which of the Collected Works are you reading now?" Naturally, I was studying many different subjects, and many different approaches to the psyche, but he knew, as I came to know, that there was so much wisdom to be found in Jung that even these decades later, we have only begun to plumb his importance.

In some way, this book had its genesis in Ireland, at Shannon Airport. I had just finished a week's educational seminar on the Dingle Peninsula. A cardiologist member of the group walked over to me as we waited for the Aer Lingus flight, and said, "Keep those little books coming. We need them, and *those questions*, too."

He was referring to some questions I had included in our seminars, questions which I consider necessary to the examined life. We recall that Socrates believed that the unexamined life was not worth living. While we might on some days prefer to simply be happy carrots, relieved of our urgencies, our anxieties and impossible desires, we also suffer greatly when we are not living the life which the psyche wishes us to live. Such existential bad faith will always demand some payment—in the body, in our relationships, in our disturbing dreams, or in the burden our children will have to carry for us.

On another occasion, after a talk in which we discussed the

idea of the examined life, a woman in the audience said, "Why should I think about these things?"

"Because," I replied, "you might be living somebody else's life if you don't."

"Why does that matter, if I am happy?"

"Possibly your soul's deepest intent is not happiness; it may rather intend that your find your journey in defeat, in exile, in the valley of suffering."

"But I wouldn't want that," she said.

"None of us do," I replied. "But your psyche desires its own ends, and will always respond; call it the will of the gods. Moreover, psyche will pathologize its violation through your body, your behavior, your storms of affect. Or possibly your children will have to carry your unlived life into their own journeys."

While I do not believe I persuaded her, I think her response is the one most of us would make. Yet our psyche has a volition, a goal, of its own quite outside the desires of the ego. What if Jesus has followed his ego need for comfort, left Gethsemane and hopped the first camel out of town? What if Beethoven had settled for being a fat sausage instead of a man who wrestled with the gods? What if Gautama Buddha had been content to live forever in the pleasure palace his parents had created for him?

What if we were to walk away from the life to which we are called? Would it be accurate, then, to say we were here, really in this life? Could we actually claim to be present? Would that avoidance not prove a violation of the needs of our soul? Many of us see ourselves in that old parable of the person sent out by a king, bearing a message, but we have forgotten. So we wander around aimlessly, not remembering that we carry the message of a king. Is there any better way to describe our condition than that we are what the Navaho call the *Chindi*, the "hungry ghosts," which wander the earth in restless search for a home, little intimating that they are already there?

It is reported that on her deathbed Gertrude Stein spoke: "What is the answer?"

She thought awhile, rose from the pillow, and said, "What is the question?"

What are the questions we need to address? That, already, is a right question, and there are many more.

One way of looking at this journey is to observe that psyche presents us with two large questions, one for the first half of life and one for the second. The question of the first half of life is essentially this: "What is the world asking of me?"

That is, what do I have to do to respond to the expectations of Mother and Father; and, later, how do I meet the demands of school, work and relationship? Our response requires the development of ego strength and an operational sense of self. We cannot know the *Self*, which is a metaphor for the organizing, purposive energies of psyche which have a life and a *telos* transcendent to consciousness. But we are challenged to gain some provisional, adaptive sense of identity in the world into which fate has thrust us.[2]

The question of the second half of life, however, is quite different: "What, now, does the soul ask of me?" When we recall that the word *psyche*, from the Greek, means "soul," then we realize that we have shifted from a biological and social agenda in the first half of life, to a psychological and spiritual agenda in the second half.[3]

Each of these questions is necessary for the development of personhood. First comes ego development and social participation, then comes the relocation of the ego in a larger context, a reframing by and in response to what is transcendent to the ego's limited capacity. The person who has reached midlife and

---

[2] That our "sense of self" is often false, an adaptive strategy that in time becomes a constrictive prison which limits our development, is a subject I explored in *The Middle Passage: From Misery to Meaning at Midlife.*
[3] The expression "half of life" is meant metaphorically here, for what stuns or guides a person into the second categorical question will vary, depending on the person and the circumstances. It is a change in focus that often occurs in one's late thirties or early forties, but may happen at any time.

still not created an ego identity, and a stake in the social context, has much unfinished business. But the person who clings to the values and idols of the first half—youth, status, continuous reassurance from others—is locked into a regressive and self-alienating pattern in which he or she colludes in the violation of their soul and their summons. Thus, not only do we have questions, but life has questions for us.

In the second half of life, whether through volition or necessity, we become obliged to read surfaces in order to go beneath surfaces, which is to say, become psychological beings. A psychological being is one who asks, what is going on here, what causes this, from whence in my history, or the history of the other, does this arise? Not to ask such questions is to be at the mercy of the autonomous, affect-laden ideas that Jung called *complexes*. These are energy clusters which have a life of their own and, when unchallenged, put one's life on automatic pilot. Our ego identities are often hard won in the face of our own great intrapsychic regressive tendencies, our longing for sleep and satiety of spirit, as well as the vagaries and vicissitudes of a demanding external environment.

Naturally, we do not take the usurpation of conscious control lightly, yet it occurs moment to moment in our lives. This gives rise to patterns derived from the looping contents of complexes and their reflexive world views When we acknowledge the power of our genetic and cultural coding, and the autonomous clusters of programmed and re-programming energy at work within us, the range of free choice seems limited indeed. Whatever freedom of choice is possible, we can only reach it when we have reflected on these autonomous histories within.

I am persuaded that the chief goal of the second half of life, and that of therapy by the way, is to make one's life as interesting as possible. That seems a modest claim, especially for a person in deep pain, yet our lives are an unfolding mystery, only partly in our control, in which we are not only the protagonist, but often the most amazed of witnesses. No matter how small our role, each of us is a carrier of cosmic energy and a crucial part of a great, unfolding pattern. We will not see the end of that pattern, but we need to carry our own part of it to the end. No mosaic exists without its separate, brilliant fragments. Something is living us, even more than we are living it. As a child, you knew this; as an adult you must remember it.

Your story is enfolded within the world story, and the world story is wrapped around your private story. The moral and spiritual texture of each story is the progressive embodiment of a set of questions, some conscious, some unconscious. The more consciously we address the questions of our lives, the more we will experience our lives as meaningful.

As children we necessarily had to ask, explicitly and implicitly, What do my parents want from me? What does the world want of me? How can I best survive, meet my needs? The questions our life is organized around will either enlarge or diminish it. If in the second half of life our questions are: How can I be financially secure? How can I find someone to take care of me? How can I get people to like me? Then our lives will be diminished because, as natural and understandable as these concerns are, they are too small for the agenda of the soul. As Jung said, we walk in "shoes too small."[4]

Walking in shoes too small, we live in lives too small. If the question our parents enacted for us was, "How can we get our neighbors to like us?" chances are that we learned to be jugglers, tricksters, *bricoleurs*, those who twist and turn and deflect and divert in the solicitation of approval. How would such an agenda ever redeem us from childhood dependency? If their question was "How do we find security?" chances are our current lives are fear-based even while, no matter what we do, security seems further and further away. If their question was "How can we avoid

---

[4] "Analytical Psychology and 'Weltanschauung,' " *The Structure and Dynamics of the Psyche,* CW 8, par. 739. [CW refers throughout to *The Collected Works of C.G. Jung]*

offending God?" then we have most likely come to offend God most by not becoming our own selves, that experiment which Divinity attempts through us.

The implicit question our family of origin lived became ours by internalization and assimilation, and, next to our genetics—also received from parents, of course—is the single most formative influence on our personal psychology.

Privately we may have had other questions as children, the right questions as it were, but their expression was a luxury seldom encouraged by the environment. I recall as a child asking, "What does it all mean?" I imagined that the cloud-capped vault of the skies above formed a cell, that that cell was part of the brain of a great thinker, and that I and the world were but a thought of that thinker, a sort of cosmic musing. It also occurred to me, with an existential *frisson*, that said thinker might have another thought, another whim, and we would all vanish.

Strangely, I felt afraid to tell anyone else of my vision for I feared ridicule. But I was not frightened by this picture; rather, I was fascinated by it. Even though it leant an air of insubstantiality to the world, it did address, if not answer, my deepest questions. "Why this thought, this dream, this life?" The metaphor of a cosmic thinker allowed, demanded, the deepening of the question, and promised still more mystery in its infinite regressions. This kind of question is life at its most interesting. All children spontaneously ask such questions, produce such images, but we learn to set them aside; thus, in time, the world loses its luster and deteriorates into quotidian monotony.

How I warmed later to the opening section of James Agee's *A Death in the Family,* where he writes: "We are talking now of summer evenings in Knoxville, Tennessee, in the time that I lived there so successfully disguised to myself as a child."[5]

Rufus, the child, lying on the grass after the evening meal, is present, as we all were, to the largeness of the journey, and his

---

[5] *A Death in the Family,* p. 11.

sensibility is attuned to the timeless drama of those crepuscular skies. His body is that of a contingent child; his imaginal soul participates in something larger than this time, this place, this Nashville. He wonders, what has brought all of them together in this convergence of mysteries:

> By some chance here they are, all on this earth; and who shall ever tell the sorrow of being on this earth, lying on quilts, on the grass, in a summer evening, among the sounds of night . . . ? After a little I am taken in and put to bed . . . and those receive me, who quietly treat me, as one familiar and well beloved in that home; but will not, oh, will not, not now, not ever; tell me who I am.[6]

For this child, for all of us, the question is "Who am I?" Yes, he is his mother's son, his father's orphan, but the question is to be worked out at some level deeper than conscious autobiography can contain.

For those whose temperament and calling inclines them toward engineering, systems analysis, troubleshooting, their prevailing question in childhood is: "How does it work?" For the pragmatist, for whom ideas are tools, the question may be: "What are the consequences?" or "How *well* does it work?" To those of aesthetic sensibility, the question is "What is its texture?" "Why does that color affect me so deeply?" All of these questions are aspects of our primal wonder, and suggest a desire to go beneath the surface to the heart of things, to discern the movement of the invisible.

But if my adult question is "How can I be secure?" or "How can I fit in?" or "How can I find protective love?" or "How can I be liked by others?" then I shall be enslaved to the uncertain response of the world. Whenever we transfer the authority of instinct and intuition to our external environment, often as a result of childhood vulnerability and dependence, we remain thereafter at its mercy. As a colleague once said to a wrangling couple, "In your relationship you sacrificed your independence

---

[6] Ibid., p. 15.

to gain security, and ended up with neither." As we are fragile beings, vulnerable and in the end alone, the search for security is understandable, but when it prevails over everything, the depth and scope of life is diminished.

For example, as an adult James Agee returned to the pivotal event of his childhood—the death of his father in an auto accident—and sought to reconstruct its meaning. He wrote and rewrote the manuscript at least seven times and was still not finished when death took him in 1955. As important as his father's death was, his central question remained, "Who am I?"

The huge impact of the loss of a parent is immeasurable, but the child is more than even this loss. We are all more than the sum of what has happened to us. In speaking recently with a woman undergoing a divorce, a frightening and lonely time to be sure, we concluded together that it was *only* her marriage. Her life is something larger, of which the current travail is an important part. But the meaning of that life will be how these days are metabolized, and how and to what degree she outgrows the tyranny of her abandonment fears.

The poet Rainer Maria Rilke also explored his recollection of childhood. He recalled the lost playground of Prague and his friends. Their spontaneous enthusiasm, their innocence, their raucous exuberance, had been slowly effaced by the years, eroded by adult gravities and the pressure of ominous events. Yet Rilke still asks what was real in that flood of sensations, that concatenation of shouted emotion, that flush and flurry of flung bodies? He asks because he is also asking this large question in the present. Whoever does not sort and sift the detritus of daily life is living unconsciously.

> What was real in all of that?
> Nothing. Only the balls, with their wonderful curves.
> Not even the children . . . yet sometimes one of them,
> O fleeting child, stepped under a falling ball.[7]

---

[7] *Sonnets to Orpheus,* II, 8 (author's translation).

With marvelous economy, Rilke is able to summon up the affect tied to the images which memory provides, and to conjure, through metonymy, a figure associated with some larger theater of events. The ball at the heart of so many childhood games serves not only as literal memory, but also as intuitive apprehension of the curve of time and space back upon itself. The ball, thrown ever so high, ever so far, will, must, always return to earth; so, too, these precious, fragile, mortal children, gravity-bound aspirants to heaven. The ball soars through the skies in the timeless hall of Rilkean memory, but as it falls to earth its saturnine shadow sometimes falls on those golden children.

In his selection of the metonymical ball, Rilke succeeds not only in the re-collection of childhood, but in opening an aperture to that mortal curve which guides us all. Forever flung heavenward, we curve forever to ground. Those children—poised between being and death, vulnerable, afraid, fearless, innocent, unconscious, and intuiting eternity—what could they know? Play for them was worship, simply Being. Yet what the child did not know consciously, the adult re-collects in this moment where we walk, perchance, beneath the falling ball, and step unwitting into its curving career. This is our mystery, and to forget it is to live a trivial life.

Recall those moments, back then, when you were by yourself, in the back yard, in a tree, in your room. What did you think? What images rose as creatures from your own depths? What questions haunted you? As you lay in bed at night, what fears lurked beneath the bed? (By day, my brother and I raced by pulling ourselves by the mattress springs, amid the dust bunnies, in the never-ending heats of childhood Olympiads. By night, alligators lurked beneath the same beds. No matter that no alligator had ever been seen in Illinois, they were surely there, waiting to snap off the dangling leg of a careless boy).

Events then hurtled toward us like next summer, but we could not see them. How poised we are to see the past, now, but could not then see the other side of time, our precocious plummet toward the future, where gifts and losses, pains and pleasures, griefs and joys rushed toward collision. Oh the wonder of it all. The wonder and the terror forgotten, buried but not dead, beneath the details of the daily round. As our bodies grew large, the world demanded and we, perforce, complied. And so we forgot those questions, and who we were, and that we were really called upon to do something with this gift of life.

In later years, one surveys the wreckage, a history which sometimes ennobles, sometimes degrades, but always, always, humbles.

By now we know that parents could no more help us than they could save themselves, nor could the brittle teachers, the ministers with oleaginous smiles, the whore politicians. No one did, or could, or does, not then, not during, not now. So you have to pause, to figure things out for yourself. What is not conscious owns you, and very little is conscious, even with earnest effort. Jung challenges us: "Man's worst sin is unconsciousness, but it is indulged in with the greatest piety even by those who should serve mankind as teachers and examples."[8]

This is a sin of which we are all guilty. Possibly the first step away from it is to confess that not only did we not get the life we expected, or intended, but that other forces were at work within us, making choices, creating patterns, subverting or serving our ancient destiny. Some of those patterns were created by the autonomous powers of the old complexes, with their invisible filaments reaching down into history and replicating its dynamics if not its surface appearances.

We also know that something large was intending itself through us, and when the world imposed itself, or we chose wrongly, it was wounded and expressed its anguish in body or affect, in dream or behavior. All this time, not only were the complexes complicating our lives, but the Self was *selving*. We

---

[8] "The Phenomenology of the Spirit in Fairytales," *The Archetypes and the Collective Unconscious,* CW 9i, par. 455.

know now that we do not make our story; our story makes us. As Jung observed, "It is not I who create myself, rather I happen to myself."[9]

What follows here are ten chapters, ten questions, the addressing of which, to my mind, deepens the character of our journeys. I do not purport to offer their answers, though I present possibilities. These are not the only questions worthy to be included, but they are those which presently seem to me to be most useful. As Rilke wrote to a young friend, we should not expect the answers immediately:

> Be patient toward all that is unsolved in your heart and . . . try to love the *questions themselves* like locked rooms and like books that are written in a very foreign tongue. Do not now seek the answers, which cannot be given you because you would not be able to live them. And the point is, to live everything. *Live* the questions now. Perhaps you will then gradually, without noticing it, live along some distant day into the answers.[10]

So we are obliged to live the questions, with whatever courage we can muster. And then, as Rilke noted, we may live our way along into their answers.

---

[9] "Transformation Symbolism in the Mass," *Psychology and Religion*, CW 11, par. 391.
[10] *Letters to a Young Poet*, p. 35.

1
By What Truths Am I living My Life?

By what autonomous, mythological truths am I living my life, or better, which are living me? This is a question generally ignored by philosophy, theology and even most modern psychology.

When I took my first college philosophy course I was naïve enough to think that by studying the great philosophers I could learn the nature of truth. Surely, I imagined, Plato and Aristotle, Kant and Nietzsche, Russell and Wittgenstein had superior minds and had things figured out. This naiveté is embarrassing today. But even at the time, it did not take me very long to learn that their chief gift would be to cause me to replace the idea of "truth" with the idea of "truths," and, upon further reflection, to give up the thought of truth *or* truths, and search out instead questions that were worth addressing.

I learned to value theology, how the mind and heart framed a response to the transcendent Other, or to problems such as the nature of evil. But in the end, no amount of logic or authority or tradition could persuade me if I did not have the immediate experience of the numinous. There was no such thing as proof if it was not lived.

I took my first psychology course to learn how we tick, hoping to gain some special advantage in understanding the workings of the mind. Maybe, I thought, there was "truth" in psychology.

Here again, principles of psychic functioning could be engaging or diverting, but with each course I felt farther and farther from understanding. For awhile I hoped that in time the mere sum of such courses would finally coalesce into a pyramid of knowledge that would make sense of this journey. This notion, too, proved deceptive.

While I greatly value what I learned then, today I also consider my youthful expectations a form of folly. As much as I respected philosophy, theology and psychology, I was more deeply satisfied by literature because, for me, it embodied more of the depth of human experience. In time I came to realize that most philosophy, theology and psychology was driven, as I had been, by a hidden power complex, namely the desire to know in order to control.

There is an imperialist inside each of us who wishes to conquer the world and make it one's own. Did you ever wonder why the chief language of Brazil is Portuguese while most of the rest of South America speaks Spanish? The answer is that the reigning Pope, at the height of the European exploration of the Western world, was a loyal Spaniard and ceded much greater spheres of influence to Spain than to its rival Portugal (who swallowed the lion's share of Africa). So who appointed the Vatican to be the arbiter of another civilization's destiny? Such an imperialist exists in each of us, sad to say. But instead of a continent, we usually try to control our children or our partners.

The more I studied, the further I felt from any sense of satisfaction. Only literature and the arts seemed to get close. In time I realized that these were more satisfying because they consciously employ metaphor and symbol to point in the direction of the larger mystery. They are content not to try to name them, and are more willing than the other disciplines to abide mystery and ambiguity. They embody questions rather than concrete answers that quickly become mere artifacts of ego-consciousness seeking to contain the evasive gods. (This is why so many of the examples I give in my books are from literature and the arts rather than from clinical practice.)

Of all branches of learning, the easiest for me to master conceptually was psychology, which today defines the human being as a series of behaviors, cognitions and psychopharmacological processes. The measuring and the manipulation of each of these modalities is a matter of relative ease, all in service of course to the fantasy of control—controlling ourselves or controlling others. (As Freud said in a revealing slip of his own, where Id is, there Ego shall be). In this fragmenting of the human soul, modern psychology and psychiatry fall far short of approaching the mystery of human nature. Nonetheless, the implicit fantasy which contemporary psychology serves is to bring the world under the domination of the conscious mind, even though each of us really knows better. One behavioral psychologist admitted to me, as we began our first analytic session, "You know, when we do our own therapy we choose a psychodynamic approach." His work, on behalf of his clients and their insurance companies, was no doubt conscientious, but it was also insufficient, as he knew when it came to addressing his own journey.

Take all the insights of philosophy, theology and psychology, great as they are, and one is still left with the mystery of who we are, what we are driven by and what we serve.

When we can relinquish our fantasy of control through understanding, and accept that we are a mystery, that some large life courses within us with its own goal, then we live closer to the heart of things. When we can admit that there are autonomous energies which spin forth our lives, then we are appropriately humbled by their power, their inaccessibility and their essential otherness. We err to make them mere artifacts of consciousness; rather, consciousness is an epiphenomenon of these energies, and more often than not their servant. As Jung said time and again, whoever has discovered the power of the unconscious knows thereafter that he is not the master in his own house.

Acknowledging that I am not the master in my own house may humble and dismay me, but at least I am then back in the place where I am meant to be—standing before the large rather than the small. Whatever becomes an artifact of consciousness is diminished. When, on the other hand, consciousness is confronted by all that is not conscious, it is enlarged. It is enlarged not by its mastery, its control, but by the magnitude of the mystery with which it is engaged in dialectical relationship.

Of the many contributions Jung has made to our understanding, few exceed the concept of the complex. The word itself has entered popular culture to the point that it would be wrong to belabor the obvious here. But the radical role of the complex in our lives is underestimated by that same popular culture. It is the chief delusion of the ego that it knows, that it is in control, when in fact it almost blindly serves some autonomous quasi-mythological fragment. Only in a moment of phenomenological response, a startle, a sudden spontaneity, such as when we are struck by the cold water of a morning shower, are we truly in this moment. Most of the time we serve whatever charged history fate has provided.

A complex is a mythological subsystem that is the result of the accretion of personal experience around a certain idea. We have complexes because we have a history. As Jung noted,

> The possession of complexes does not in itself signify neurosis . . . and the fact that they are painful is no proof of pathological disturbance. Suffering is not an illness; it is the normal counterpole to happiness. A complex becomes pathological only when we think we have not got it.[11]

In each of these historically charged fragments there is an implicit idea. When Jung called them feeling-toned responses to life, he was emphasizing that each core idea is charged with affect. And such affect is itself the embodiment of an idea that the psyche has provisionally formed around the experience. Learning to decipher that implicit idea is a chief task of reflection and of psychotherapy.

But the complex is also a picture of that situation, an image incarnate. Jung says that a complex

> is the *image* of a certain psychic situation which is strongly accentuated emotionally and is, moreover, incompatible with the habitual attitude of consciousness.[12]

---

[11] "Psychotherapy and a Philosophy of Life," *The Practice of Psychotherapy,* CW 16, par. 179.

[12] "A Review of the Complex Theory," *The Structure and Dynamics of the Psyche,* CW 8, par. 201.

As an image of experience, a complex is a translation, an embodiment of the invisible. Only when the invisible becomes manifest as image can we discern and track it. One venue for incarnation is the body, a portion of which seizes up when a complex is activated. Or it may be a pattern of behavior which leaves a complex, variable trail—not unlike the wake of a half-submerged water creature.

We can see why behavior modification is so tempting. It addresses the image, the behavior, and seeks to replace it with other behaviors. Also, we can see why cognitive psychology is so appealing because it seeks to change the implicit idea behind the manifestation. But neither addresses the underlying mythology, that is, the conversion of a lived experience into a feeling, an idea, a behavior and a value system whose source lies beneath consciousness altogether.

Thus, the fantasy of gaining control over this deep source, as psychology claims, is itself a complex, a complex triggered by our anxiety at being in the presence of the inexplicable, the intractable, the invisible.

Analogously, no matter how sincere our theologies, our beliefs, may be, however grounded in primal experience, the gods slip away from original creed and ritual to undermine consciousness by changing their shape, moving deeper and reappearing somewhere else in a different guise.

Unfortunately, as many of us know, simply being aware of a complex does not render it harmless, for the affective charge it bears continues to discharge long after initial recognition. Complexes, writes Jung,

> interfere with the intentions of the will and disturb the conscious performance; . . . they appear and disappear according to their own laws; . . . in a word, complexes behave like independent beings.[13]

Having called them "splinter psyches," Jung notes that often

---

[13] "Psychological Factors in Human Behaviour," ibid., par. 253.

complexes derive from internal moral conflict, "which ultimately derives from the apparent impossibility of affirming the
whole of one's nature."[14] This sort of conflict is especially interesting in the second half of life when we wish to take more
conscious responsibility for the conduct of our lives. We are,
thus, multiple, competing value systems. No wonder we are such
contradictory creatures to live with.

When the values are derived from an historically charged experience—and when are they not?—then we are potentially in
the grip of past choices. Those choices were often dictated by
surrounding circumstances; thus their values are of another time
and place, often from moments less empowering and less conscious, not from this moment with its larger set of options. The
historical authenticity of these value systems is what occasions
the repetitions in our lives, and is most disconcerting to one who
would be free to choose his or her own journey.

An awakened consciousness of such splinter mythological systems is only part of their resolution. Complexes, as such, do not
go away, for they are our history, but they can be superseded by
other, more empowering complexes, or have their energy redis-
tributed to the realm of the ego. Yet, Jung is wise to suggest that,
paradoxically, the path toward greater freedom is to be found
through, not around, those complexes:

> A complex can be really overcome only if it is lived out to the full.
> In other words, if we are to develop further we have to draw to us
> and drink down to the very dregs what, because of our complexes,
> we have held at a distance.[15]

What can this mean? Jung is inviting each person to an enlarging acceptance of what is a *de facto* moral conflict, a value
split, and to live the split and the competing moral values more
consciously. This advice is indeed contrary to the implied opti-

---

[14] "A Review of the Complex Theory," ibid., par. 204.
[15] "Psychological Aspects of the Mother Archetype," *The Archetypes and the
Collective Unconscious,* CW 9i, par. 184.

mism of behavioral and cognitive psychologies. In the Jungian approach to therapy, the task is not the elimination of complexes, as if that were even possible, but redemption by honoring their power and autonomy.

That is what makes depth psychology so demanding. We would prefer to have our complexes removed by the therapist-surgeon; we wish our moral conflict anaesthetized; we wish to transcend our own history, not drag its values into each new moment of our lives.

To drink the complex to the dregs, as Jung suggests, is to suffer greatly. When we ask where we are most stuck in our lives, no doubt a large moral agenda will surface. Why are we stuck? We are stuck because beneath the surface of any issue is a set of filaments which invisibly lead back to an earlier place. To become unstuck, we will once again have to take on the affective charge of that issue, suffering the return of the value-laden lens of an earlier, disempowered time. No wonder we would rather resist growth. W.H. Auden noted:

> We would rather be ruined than changed.
> We would rather die in our dread
> Than climb the cross of the present
> And let our illusions die.[16]

Auden too sees the intractability of our history. How could we choose ruin over change, or to die in our dread? The answer lies in being so intimidated by the barely intuited fear of the largeness the present asks of us, and by the dislocation of the old values (however negative they may be), that we would rather choose stasis, replicative history, old dread rather than new angst. Thus, Jung's admonition to go through the complex makes the only sense. Whatsoever we fear becomes the agenda for growth. If one is blocked by the disempowering value system of the past, precisely that value system is to be suffered and con-

---

[16] "The Age of Anxiety," in *Collected Poems,* p. 407.

fronted by conscious choice and by committed carry-through.

Talk is cheap; such sustained commitment is extraordinarily difficult. It helps when one realizes that the voice of the past is often archaic and whispers our most primitive fears. "If I act so and so, I will lose your affection." "If I speak my own mind, you will punish me." For the child we once were, such outcomes were potentially devastating, which is what gives the issues so much energy. That these outcomes are now unlikely is not as important as the recognition that a life of integrity requires that in this world, in this time and place, I must learn to choose rather than submit to the dictates of archaic fears.

Relating directly to the fear is an act of great liberation. The person we have become, or wish to be, is capable of action in the face of such archaic fears. We become the person we wish to be precisely by making choices in the face of fear. The "cross of the present" threatens to dismember us with its contradictory value systems, but the dynamism of such an intersection pushes one to the third possibility. The "third" is enlargement through containing the opposites. We have already agreed that we cannot leave the values of history in the past; we can only transcend their tyranny through a psychological tenacity which chooses differently: "If I risk myself, I may lose your approval. If I lose your approval, I will perhaps still be larger, for I will have gained my own approval."

One woman literally clutched her throat when she was about to speak some deep personal truth. The old monitor had functioned autonomously so long she was not aware of this outer manifestation of a self-protective complex. Once it was identified, she knew she had a task. She risked speaking more directly to her husband, to her friends, to her therapist, and found that the world did not collapse, that she was newly respected, and that some old wound had healed within her. Today the gesture of self-censorship begins, is caught, she swallows deeply, and she speaks. And her world is larger.

So what are the truths which we are living, or which are living us? Wheresoever patterns are found, there are complexes at work. Wheresoever complexes are found, history prevails over the present. Wheresoever history prevails over the present, we are stuck. Wheresoever we are stuck, there is a moral task. Wheresoever there is a moral task, we will be obliged to take on some quantum of anxiety. Wheresoever we are willing to take on anxiety, we will grow and create new patterns, new history. Wheresoever we choose newly in the present, we render our journey more conscious, larger, and possibly more consistent with what destiny demands.

Teasing out the implicit message embodied in every complex is difficult but possible. What was overwhelming to the child can be borne by the adult if he or she has grown in consciousness. Because the wiring beneath the surface connects to the archaic anxiety, we shut down the present and reflexively respond out of the world view that was historically programmed. Nonetheless, as we have grown larger, we are able to endure such anxiety, especially if we realize that giving in will result in the loss of our purchase on the present, our personal integrity and our freedom.

Once a complex is consciously related to, is it likely that an adult would still succumb to repetitive behavior patterns? No, not likely, but inevitable. Alas, complexes are deeply wired, so we are often caught in their intricate web.

Jung expressed this mechanism thus: "When an inner situation is not made conscious, it happens outside, as fate."[17] This simple sentence contains as much wisdom as ancient Greek tragedy. In fact, Greek tragedy was implicitly based on this dynamic. What I do not know within myself will be making choices for me, and yet I will discern that such events came rushing toward me from outside. I will identify as Fate what I have unwittingly chosen.

Three examples may suffice to illustrate the richness of Jung's conflation of the limits of consciousness and the ministries of Fate.

---

[17] "Christ: A Symbol of the Self," *Aion,* CW 9ii, par. 126

1. Leftover needs from childhood will generally oblige one to be attracted to a person who will ostensibly fulfill those needs, or, just as often, repeat their disappointment.

Thus, one's intimate relationships are predicated on the old wound, the unhealthful template, rather than the healthy dialectical engagement with the other.[18] We have a powerful tendency to repeat the dynamics of prior relationships, especially those with Mother and Father, our first, most powerful lessons in the interactive strategies of self and other. Because the outer world always seems different, and is, we are unaware of the dynamics which course below the surface. Hence one tends toward the fulfillment of the original template, with its predictable, fractious and disappointing outcomes. Little knowing we have chosen that other specifically for repetition, we will likely blame him or her for our unconsciousness. Fate brought us together, we wish to argue, and all the while we recreated choices from hidden places.

2. Substantial wounds, or the inherent traumata of life, may fixate growth and thereby limit the range of choices we can imagine. Accordingly, we chose from a narrower portion of the spectrum than is in fact available to us in the present, constricting our own potential. If early trauma has usurped the ego's powers of reflection, one lies locked within a so-called personality disorder, a disordered relationship to self. While we all have some disorders of self-relationship, those deeply wounded in this way are usually unable to reflect psychologically or morally, and thus can only repeat a very limited range of behaviors.

The limits of both family of origin and culture narrow the range of our freedom. Education and the encounter with other cultures reveal the limited range of our personal experience, and often open us to different values, new possibilities. As children are limited or emboldened by the expectations that others communicate to them, so each of us is limited by the narrow lens of

---

[18] See Hollis, *The Eden Project: In Search of the Magical Other,* for a lengthier discussion of the psychodynamics of relationship.

our complexes. No wonder we tend to repeat our lives, and that of our parents, unless the imaginal spectrum has been expanded to include more than that with which we were earlier gifted.

When trauma rather than cultural exposure plays the limiting role, the power of the fixation is greater. The undoing of that fixation will always oblige some form of what Freud called the task of therapy—re-education of the complexes.

3. We identify with the values and range of possibilities presented to us by our cultural context. Thus, as we absorb the implicit message that materialism is the best treatment for our spiritual poverty, so we will remain dis-eased and unhappy even when we have achieved what we desired. Our objects will own us then, and we will need to enslave ourselves further in order to maintain them and add to them.

One thoughtful person said to me recently that few people are interested in the work that therapy requires. They are mostly interested in money and good health. Both values become idols and estrange the individual ever further. It is not that health is wrong, of course, it is what value we transfer to it. When health obliges repeated cosmetic surgery and disfigurement, when we use it to deny aging and mortality, when it fixates us in a bodily state which is a denial of our condition, then it is neurotic. If obsessions with money and health worked, we would know it. They are cultural complexes from which none of us is wholly free. And each of us is in part owned by what is not rendered fully conscious. How could we argue that we are free, then, or living our journey when we are in fact prisoners of that most transient of realities, the fevers and fashions of popular culture?

These are the kinds of complex mythologies that own us, and from which freedom may only be acquired if we open to the challenge of other questions. So, what are the questions that might help us unravel this larger question: "By what truths am I living my life, or which are living me?"

Here are some of them. Ask them long enough, with sincerity, and they will take you to a different place in your journey.

Where are your patterns?

Where do you feel stuck?

What anxiety is aroused when you contemplate alternatives?

What specific fears can be unpacked from the much vaguer but paralyzing angst?

Which of those fears is based on childhood experience, with its limited powers and its limited awareness of a larger world?

Which of those fears are indeed likely to happen?

Can you bear them happening?

What will happen to you if you do not bear them, and you stay stuck?

Can you risk being a larger person?

Can you bear the pain of growth over the pain of remaining afraid, small and lost?

Can you accept that, at the end of your life, you were not really here?

Can you bear to have been only a hungry ghost, a victim of fate, a refugee from destiny?

Can you bear having been only a troubled guest on this earth without making some part of it yours?

Can you face these questions?

Can you live with yourself not facing these questions, now that you know they exist?

Can these questions recover your journey for you?

Can they, can you?

> And so long as you haven't experienced
> This: to die and so to grow,
> You are only a troubled guest
> On the dark earth.[19]

---

[19] J.W. von Goethe, "The Holy Longing," in Robert Bly, James Hillman and Michael Meade, eds., *The Rag and Bone Shop of the Heart: Poems for Men*, p. 382.

2
What Is My Shadow and
How Can I Make It Known?

Among the most useful, if most misunderstood, of Jung's contributions to psychology is the idea of the shadow. Simply put, the shadow is everything about myself with which I am uncomfortable. I may not be conscious of my shadow, or I may not wish to be conscious of it. It is that which unsettles me, undermines my conscious values, or would oblige me to confront my values in a more conscious, sometimes embarrassing way. It is whatever I do not wish to be. Thus, in Jung's words,

> The shadow is a moral problem that challenges the whole ego-personality, for no one can become conscious of the shadow without considerable moral effort. To become conscious of it involves recognizing the dark aspects of the personality as present and real.[20]

The shadow is not synonymous with evil, though evil on personal, collective and archetypal levels are the venues in which shadow most often confronts our conscious hopes for conflict resolution, peace and justice. The problem of evil, personal or cosmic, the larger, compelling questions of theodicy—the shadow of our *imago Dei*—and sociopathy, our systemic evils, are beyond the scope of this book.

We embody our shadow in at least four different ways:

First, when it remains unconscious it makes choices for us.

Second, we project it onto others and repudiate in them what is intolerably so close to home.

Third, we identify with it and live it out, unable to critique ourselves or the consequences.

Fourth, we admit that that which makes us uncomfortable is,

---

[20] "The Shadow," *Aion,* CW 9ii, par. 14.

nonetheless, ours, so we grow in our capacity to work with its energies and consciously assimilate them.

We learn of the shadow in many ways. We receive feedback from our loved ones. We learn the hard way that disproportionate emotional reactions to small provocations is always the sign of a complex, and often indicates a shadow issue. We examine our mistakes, patterns, disconnections to see where hidden motives may be present. We examine the content and dynamics of failed expectations to see what in ourselves was projected onto the other. And we find our shadow frequently waiting for us in our dreams where the ego has no powers of censorship. Repressed energies and hidden agendas which disturb the ego's sense of itself show up in dreams and fantasies and then, once conscious, become a problem for ego to confront. Though we do not create our dreams, it would seem that, in the end, we are responsible for their contents. The first-century Roman poet Terence's observation that nothing human is alien to us remains the best, humbling reminder that what is wrong in the world, wrong in others, is wrong in each of us as well.

As we mature, we acquire a growing capacity to include shadow, to contain more opposites, to accept those parts of ourselves we have not liked. The more mature our consciousness, the more opposites we are asked to acknowledge without repudiation, and the more is asked of ego for conscious, ethical choices. Liliane Frey-Rohn has expressed this paradox succinctly: " 'Too much morality' strengthens evil in the inner world, and 'too little morality' promotes a dissociation between good and evil."[21] The shabby comportment of contemporary moral vigilantes embodies the former imbalance, and the currency of unconscious acting out in personal and public life embodies the latter.

As unconscious as we may be in our behavior, even when we do evil, perhaps the shadow is nowhere more influential than in

---

[21] "Evil from a Psychological Point of View," in *Spring 1965.*

our unlived lives. As infants, later children, we learn to dissociate from our natural selves, our best selves, because their enactment is too costly. From early days in the family of origin, every child receives and internalizes such implied messages as: "My laughter stirs up mother's anxiety," "My independent opinion is resented by my father," "My deepest feelings are traded for security."

What child has not made compromises to gain acceptance and domestic tranquility? Not only have we internalized the unconscious needs of others—"this is the way to live"—but we have grown highly skilled in "reading" their slightest reaction, or nuance of voice, and then swallowing the shame that follows each of our Quisling accommodations. Over time, who has not come to identify with these defensive mechanisms? Who has not carried a baggage of depression, of rage, of shame ever since? And who is not now, as an adult, still enacting the required compromises of the child?

The price of accommodations for acceptance, approval and the management of angst is the loss of instinctual wholeness, that is, neurosis. Our shadow is at the core of our neuroses, which are in large part symptomatic of our estrangement from the Self, our guiding center. Writes Jung:

> Analytic psychology is a reaction against the exaggerated rationalization of consciousness which, seeking to control nature, isolates itself from her and so robs man of his own natural history.[22]

Elsewhere he says that neurotic suffering "is an unconscious fraud and has no real merit, as has real suffering."[23]

Often our unlived life surfaces at key moments, as in the projection of our contrasexual others—anima or animus—in a love affair, or in an intractable depression, or in a sudden enantiodromia which sends one off on an urgent, compulsive shift in

---

[22] "Analytical Psychology and 'Weltanschauung,' " *The Structure and Dynamics of the Psyche,* CW 8, par. 739.
[23] "Analytical Psychology and Education," *The Development of Personality,* CW 17, par. 154.

one's life course. It is a frequent component in the dynamics of couples, where blame is so easy to lay on the other, while ignoring the fact that one chose precisely that very person to be the carrier of one's shadow. The places of attraction are often the places of conflict and repetition, so it becomes very difficult to discern what is within ourselves and what belongs to the other. Many marital quarrels, then, are in fact a *folie à deux*, an unwitting participation in a shadow dance in which each has a familiar role, with a familiar partner, with familiar outcomes.

Since the shadow resides mostly in the unconscious, teasing it out is inherently difficult. It becomes a Chinese puzzle box: "Tell me now, of what are you unconscious?" Yet what is unconscious owns us, and often injures those in our care or sphere of influence. Add to that the ego's tendency to dissociate from that which is uncomfortable or challenging. No wonder, then, that the shadow is so elusive.

In service to the possibility, indeed the heroic intention, of taking the shadow seriously, I offer the following seven questions. A conscientious wrestling with them may increase our knowledge of those parts of ourselves that other parts, also of ourselves, wish not to know.

Seven Questions for Personal Reflection on the Shadow

1. What do you consider your virtues? Can you imagine where they subvert your intentions? Can you imagine their opposites in your unconscious? Where do those opposites manifest in your outer life?

Probably each of us would describe ourselves as generally virtuous, or at least striving to be so. Most days, a self-aggrandizing list of our virtues is readily available. However, when anything is carried to its extreme—becoming one-sided and automatic—it has the potential for being dogmatic, even, in time, demonic. Prudence becomes cowardice in the face of alternatives; frugality becomes miserliness; good naturedness leads to exploitation; righteousness can cross the line into sanctimoniousness; accommodation leads to loss of integrity, and so on. As long as choices are not consciously and freshly made in contexts which are constantly shifting, virtue may prove unvirtuous.

When virtue, or right intentions, are automatic, we may be sure that the shadow of virtue is present in the unconscious. We are told that the road to Hell is paved with good intentions. How can that be? In fact, we cannot know where the ripples of our choices end, whom they affect or what other values may be violated in that separate context.

For those of us privileged to live in the so-called First World, our virtues are continuously proclaimed even as we live on the back of Second and Third World nations. What child is laboring in a sweatshop to produce my sneakers? What family is shattered by the refusal of American pharmaceuticals to share life-saving formulae? Who has been hurt by my self-righteousness? Where has the shadow of unintended consequences of my virtues shown up in family life, in business, in politics, through my projections, my transferential relationships, my one-sidedness?

Such considerations require heroic and subtle self-examination, and often prove morally vertiginous. Choice is always complicated, because hidden agendas discolor conscious oversight, even when the choices seem easy.

2. What are the key patterns of your relationships? That is to say, where does the shadow manifest itself such as in patterns of avoidance or in repetitions which bring predictably negative consequences?

The covert agenda of unmet needs insidiously burdens relationships. Most relationships fail because we ask too much of them. The narcissistic wounds which are the inevitable result of one's history return as inordinate expectations, inappropriate strategies and regressive scenarios. With such dynamics, how could one not expect repetition?

Where life was painful for the child, just there will we dialogue as adults. And where truth may not be told, the foundation is rotten. Where life was insufficient, we will be needy, controlling, manipulative. As Jung has noted, "Where love reigns, there is no will to power; and where the will to power is paramount, love is lacking."[24] If a couple could be psychologically seen at the altar, photographed in the way late nineteenth-century spiritualists sought to capture the soul leaving the body, one would observe swirling clouds and astral rays in the space between the two.

The recriminations we bring to our partners can only be balanced by the ability to see what we too have done. Achieving a reasonably healthy relationship requires a modicum of grace and a large measure of willingness to be humbled by one's own trailing cloud of shadowy material. No wonder, then, that so many are obsessed with relationships, and keenly disappointed when they don't work out.

As long as we are unconscious of the shadowy agenda we bring to relationships, we are doomed to repetition, overcompensation or various treatment plans. Strangely, even when one's history of intimacy has been painful, there is a tendency to repeatedly choose a person with whom the old wounding will be repeated. Clearly, such a counterproductive strategy is contrary to the intent of the ego. Yet the ego, under the subtle influence of the old template, has surveyed the possibilities, targeted the potential for repetition, and locked on to it. Sometimes only years later is it evident that what seemed so different had a familiar dynamic and produced a familiar outcome.

Just as commonly, one will overcompensate and try to choose the opposite, yet even then one's choice is governed by the original experience. To find someone not like one's mother, or unlike one's father, is to be still dominated by them. The one-sidedness of the compensatory choice will result in its own problems. We select a person in the secret hope of getting it right this time. But, since in the end we cannot change the other person and can only be who we are, we have only ourselves to

---

[24] *Two Essays on Analytical Psychology,* CW 7, par. 78.

call to account when it begins to feel familiar. No wonder, then, the tenuous state of relationships.

The only way to liberate ourselves is to discern what our historic relationships were—their dynamics, their scenarios, who we were, who the other was, and how we are still in thrall to forces whose origins are past, not current. It may seem terribly reductionist, not to say humbling and disappointing, but such a knowledge greatly assists in identifying the lens through which one surveys the world, finds people to reproduce one's history, and then enacts the replication. Only through considerable self-knowledge can we make a different choice and change the course of our relational history. Taking responsibility for doing this work is in fact the best way we can love the other.

3. What annoys you about your partner? Forget your rationalizations for the moment; that person was chosen for a good reason—he or she embodies aspects of your shadow.

My wife's definition of a long-term relationship is "finding one special person whom you can annoy for a very long time." I believe she says this tongue in cheek, though I cannot be sure. Nonetheless, the fact that life's annoyances are experienced most with one's partner suggests that unless some perverse deity is at work, we have actually chosen him or her ourselves.

Why would we choose irritants? Why wouldn't we, is closer to the truth. We are not only programmed to respond to others by way of the intrapsychic imago we carry into all encounters, but the implicate mythology of those imagos seeks the repetition of the original experience. Why an abused child grows up to marry an abuser is a mystery to all, yet it happens all the time. The more powerful the programming, the greater the likelihood of repetition; the earlier in our relational history, the more unconscious is its shadowy presence. Running in the other direction, overcompensating and/or seeking to fix it in our partners are other, less powerful paradigms. As these programmed imagos are mostly unconscious, they are not only hard to detect but are all the more sovereign in influencing our selections.

How heroic it becomes—and may we say loving too—when we can acknowledge that what is repeatedly stuck in our relationships is in ourselves. Such a recognition is heroic because it requires enormous strength to take on the moral burden of one's shadow, rather than trying to convert the other into what we desire. Also, it is loving because it frees them, for the moment at least, from carrying our historic agenda.

Ironically, it is the paradox of relationship that precisely our places of attraction may also be our places of conflict. Discerning which issues lie within ourselves and which in the other, while suffering the disappointment of inordinate expectations, is always a work in progress. We are thus forever whipsawed between the pull for autonomy and the desire for intimacy, the yearning for regressive embrace and the desire for freedom.

Sometimes the other carries our shadow through our programmed repetitions of the past, and sometimes as a result of our flight from other kinds of responsibility. Where one hides behind typology, or fails to own one's feelings, or uses the other to justify stuckness in the individuation project, then the shadow is at work. That which I wish to avoid within my own range of possibility is shadow, and I give it to you, my mate, to carry. This shadow-sharing may have worked for Jack Spratt, but it cripples the rest of us.

The good news about shadow encounters in relationships is that they can become sufficiently concretized to make their dynamics conscious. Life revisits us, and what we can see now as ours is thus something which can be altered. We are never free of these programmed imagos, but consciousness adds a broader range of choice and with that the possibility of freedom from repetition. We may even conclude that something in us which wishes healing has chosen that partner with whom the repetitions occur, precisely so we may work through what the child could not. The intersection of fate and choice brings us back to the developmental task. Complain as we might, it is ours to do.

4. Where do you repeatedly undermine yourself, shoot yourself in the foot, cause yourself familiar griefs? Where do you flee from your best, riskiest self?

Our deepest irritant is of course our relationship with ourselves, the one person who shows up in every scene of the play we call our life. By the time one has reached midlife, the problem is not our inevitable wounding and disappointments. Rather, it is the fact that we have progressively identified who we are with our adaptations to our environment. That is what keeps us from the larger journey toward individuation. As the old saying has it, wherever I go, there I am. Adaptive stratagems, as necessary as they once were, become institutionalized and authoritarian. Some may still be necessary, but we must become conscious of them in order to sort wheat from chaff.

The price we pay for obedience to unconscious powers is a reduction in the possibility for wholeness. If we can affirm that we are more than what has happened to us, with all the attendant reflexive responses, then we can embark on a broader course.

The notion that one enters therapy in order to blame others is enticing but deceptive. While we need to understand the character of our influential experiences and our consequent coping strategies, the whole point is to recover the captaincy of our own journey. If one has a modicum of consciousness and moral courage in the second half of life, then blame, if blame one must, is ours alone.

5. Where are you stuck in your life, blocked in your development? What fears block your growth?

We all have stuck places, and generally we know them, yet we remain stuck. Why? Does knowledge not make it possible to become unstuck? Yes, and no.

We remain stuck because beneath the surface our stuckness is wired to a complex. When we approach that stuck place, we activate energies below the visual range, and they in turn fuel the engines of anxiety. This anxiety has the power to flood the ego and shut down alternative choices. We are not aware that this internal governance system has just usurped our lives, but we feel immediately more comfortable because it has.

This wiring, which connects anxiety with ego, always has its origin in the past, often a disempowered past. Thus, not only does the anxiety throttle the ego's current powers, but reimposes the value system of that archaic past. This circuitry, which imposes history onto the present, is why we stay stuck. And stuckness can only reinforce the regressive power of that history. Thus getting unstuck grows ever more difficult.

Hey, who said it would be easy?

By implication, getting unstuck demands that one be willing to bear the anxiety occasioned by the invisible circuitry beneath consciousness. As discussed earlier, the conversion of a generalized paralyzing angst to specific fears leads to the potential for confronting them in the present. For example, the risk of losing your approval may always arouse anxiety in me. Yet, if my life is governed by that consideration, as every child's is, then I have lost my purchase on the present and perhaps my personal integrity as well. As Jung noted, we all walk in shoes too small, diminished lives not in accord with our potential.

Our shadow, then, is found in the collusion with fear and with the self-disabling deals made by the Quisling in each of us. Better to sell out my country, or myself, than face the threat of my own largeness. Can I live with that? Can you?

6. Where do Mom and Dad still govern your life, through repetition, overcompensation or your special treatment plan?

Mom and Dad here refer to the real persons—the templates for our early assumptions about the reliability of the world, the hostile or beneficent character of nature and relationships, the attitudes and accommodations we were to adopt. Mom and Dad is also shorthand for all the other powers which held sovereignty over us in the early years. They are the ones who most taught us how to be, and therefore who to be, for good or for ill.

Who has not recognized in the present an old pattern, a tone of voice, a familiar value which one had thought was left so far behind? And who has not struggled to affirm and live out values other than those of one's origins? ("I shall become anything but my mother!") And do we not still manifest the values, spoken or implied, of one of them, or the flight from them? Who has not eaten too much, drunk too much, worried too much, run toward mindlessness as an implicit treatment plan for the past? Who is not still embodying something of their unlived life, as permission denied or compulsive compensatory agenda?

Thinking metaphorically, as we must if we are to understand both the logic and the dynamics of the unconscious, we are obliged to acknowledge that the past is not past, that the parental imagos are still here, that the old assumptions underpin our present life. Our ancestors acknowledged the presence of their own ancestors more openly. They were closer to the truth than our ideology which asserts that the past has been transcended. We have ceased to believe in ghosts, and so the spectral presences of our history are all the more autonomous. Even our increased powers over nature feed the illusion that we are free of the past and in control. We have much information, some knowledge, and little wisdom regarding these presences. This is why the ghosts run rampant in all our houses.

7. Where do you refuse to grow up, wait for certainty of vision before choosing, hope for solutions to emerge fully formed, expect rescue, or wait for a guru to make sense of it all for you?

No doubt a lesson we all carry inscribed in our bones is: "You are small and powerless, and the world is large and powerful. You just have to deal with that for the rest of your life." This is our common existential truth. It has been mediated in various ways by our families of origin, and tempered, reinforced, by other experiences, but it is the central message of our journey. The ubiquity and omnipotence of this message has become such a part of the fabric of our lives that we can ill imagine alternatives. Our fragility is an overgeneralized assumption that continuously places us in a shadow complex that says: "I do not wish to confront this disproportionate relationship to the world, this disempowerment, so I will cling to the fantasies of rescue from others, an absolutely clear set of marching orders so that I may have certainty in my choices, or expect religion or my partner or psychology to make sense of it for me. If the rescuer does not step forth, I shall continue to indict my origins, blame my ex, or seek a simpler ideology to embrace."

Fundamentalism, be it religious, political or psychological, is a flight from adulthood and appeals to many because life is so scary. If I can turn my ambiguities over to the rigidity of an either/or dogma, turn my choices over to my pastor, therapist or guru, subscribe to a mythos which rationalizes the suffering of life for me, then I will have "happiness." Such happiness, even when it is attainable, is a manifestation of the shadow for it is based on the avoidance of the mystery of the journey, its largeness, and the courage it demands. It is no crime to be fearful, but it is a crime to therefore relinquish control of our journey to someone or something else. The flight from the living gods, those who bring both terror and healing, is not piety.

When we remember that the shadow is that which I do not wish to be, the betrayal of selfhood is the inability to acknowledge that that which I do not wish to be *is* me. What the gods intend has little to do with what ego intends, and the evasion of that wholeness, of which we are all guilty, is the psychological equivalent of Original Sin. As Jung notes,

> This process of coming to terms with the Other in us is well worth while, because in this way we get to know aspects of our nature which we would not allow anybody else to show us and which we would never have admitted.[25]

The shadow, then, cannot simply be evil, for it is a requisite for the possibility of wholeness. An enlarged understanding of

---

[25] *Mysterium Coniunctionis*, CW 14, par. 706.

the Self is based on the encounter with that which challenges the ego. Moreover, Jung writes elsewhere,

> If it has been believed hitherto that the human shadow was the source of all evil, it can now be ascertained on closer investigation that the unconscious man, that is, his shadow, does not consist only of morally reprehensible tendencies, but also displays a number of good qualities, such as normal instincts, appropriate reactions, realistic insights, creative impulses, etc.[26]

For those conditioned to be reflexively good, or compliant, the flight from the shadow also becomes the flight from one's best self. A shadowless person is a contradiction in terms. One who believes that he or she has no shadow is simply superficial and unconscious, quite capable of doing very large evil—to oneself or others.

To the question, then, what is my shadow? We must answer: whatever within us we wish not to face, but which nonetheless carries the germ of our wholeness. If we wish to learn more about the shadow, we needs must look to our history, yes, but more heuristically to our present fears. Where the fears are, is the shadow's dwelling, and it renews its course in our life through sundry disguises such as projection onto others, repression of a vital part of ourselves, or as the narrowing of life—the wearing of shoes too small.

---

[26] *Aion,* CW 9ii, par. 423.

3
What Is My Myth?

When we hear the word "myth," we customarily associate it with something false. So tainted has this rich concept become that we commonly use it as a denigration. When one is asked about one's myth, the first reaction is that some inferiority is implied, as if one were knowingly serving negative values or illusions.

When I use the word myth here, what I am asserting is quite different. *Myth derives from the dramatically embodied imagos which our soul serves,* whether we know them or not, whether they are helpful or not, whether culturally imposed or individual in origin. In short, our personal myth is our implicit value system, those internalized authorities and controlling ideas that govern our life, whether we know them or not, like them or not, chose them or not.

On any given day, chances are high that much of our life is a reflexive response to the activation of these imagos. Indeed, it is quite possible to imagine a life lived mostly unconsciously, governed by reflexive responses, conditioned and reinforced over time, which create patterns and libido fixations.

For example, if we are asked what our religion is, we are likely to answer with the name of some known denomination, or to declare ourselves agnostic. But this is only the ego speaking, and only in reference to a consciously identified set of beliefs. These are often less the product of conscious choice than of other forces whose roots lie in the underworld.

To be more accurate about the nature of personal myth, one has to track every decision, every response to a stimulus, outer or inner, and then discern what value is being enacted. Such monitoring is not possible, for consciousness cannot stand outside itself, reflect upon itself, all the time. Usually, such value discernment is only possible with disciplined reflection over

48

time, and/or some sort of therapeutic analysis. Since our daily choices often have an unconscious root, we may not be able to discern the values from which they derive, though we may have a ready rationale or justification of them.

In fact, most of the time one's life serves one's complexes, those deep-seated value systems derived from another time, another place. On any given day, one is more likely than not to be reenacting a mythological system internalized from popular culture or one's family of origin. Our collective ways of understanding are conditioned by the *Zeitgeist*. Were we born to another civilization, another era, our conscious values and our conditioned reflexes would be wholly different. What we take to be a fixed, unshakable truth is merely ethnocentrism, or even a passing, fashionable idea.

Earlier it was suggested that our gods today are money and good health. This may seem laughable, but the more you reflect on it, the truer it seems. A projection upon, and longing for, money is the most active agent in the psychic arterial system of modern Western culture. We believe that money makes the world go round, brings happiness, power and fulfillment, and it even supports our fantasies of salvation. Even though we all know better, our *Zeitgeist* is such that our unsatisfied desires for home, for succor, for divinity, are projected onto paper and metal, almost without question.

After a talk I once gave on our contemporary myths, a man in the audience said that his hero was Bill Gates "because there was a truly happy man." I asked if he knew Gates personally and he replied that it was self-evident that Gates was a happy man because he was wealthy. I said I did not know him either, but I did know a lot of wealthy people who were quite miserable, so I could not equate happiness and material possessions. The man simply could not conceive that I was serious. No doubt he left the meeting scratching his head and thinking me a fool. Such is the measure of the possession of a culture by a mythologically charged imago.

Though one can critique a materialist culture, who can also claim to be against good health? Yet health too is a cultural icon, a complex. We unquestioningly seek to extend life. Why, and in service to what values? We consider good health to be a birthright, a hedge against death and a form of secular salvation. But most of the compelling figures of world religions, most of the acts of scientific and artistic creativity, and much of the meaning which enlarges us, comes out of suffering and from the steady passage toward mortality. Each of our encounters with the loss of money or health brings to the surface large questions of meaning, asks us for greater consciousness, and frequently pulls us into the place nature intends for us, whether we will or not.[27]

Whenever we dance to the seductive tune of money or health, we are living a mythological system which has little to do with the journey of the soul. But while these two imagos constitute the prevailing myth for many, there are other submyths as well.

Even more ubiquitously than money or fitness, we are bewitched by the charged imagos of our family of origin. These mythologems are loaded with primal, often unanalyzable energy, generated when we were most vulnerable, least capable of rational reflection, least aware of the possibility of alternatives. The foremost of these highly charged mythological ideas, as mentioned above, is: "The world is large and powerful, and I am not." We have all internalized this message, though with a thousand variations and strategies for survival. We seek to control the world, through learning or power, or we stay out of harm's way, or we finesse the power inequity through a thousand nuanced adaptations.

The interplay of the value systems of our culture and family of origin constitutes the operational personal myth at most moments of our lives. Given the fact that we chose neither our family of origin nor the culture into which we were born, and

---

[27] See Hollis, *Swamplands of the Soul: New Life in Dismal Places,* for extensive discussion on this theme.

that both exercise enormous power in our lives, just how much has our operational myth been "chosen"?

Our ancestors intuited these autonomous powers, and sometimes even named them. In the Greek imagination, for example, such formative forces had a virtual personality: *Moira,* fate; *Dike,* justice; *Nemesis,* retribution; *Sophrosyne,* compensation; *Proerismos,* destiny. These great implacable powers opposed and often thwarted the unfolding of one's destiny. Moreover, the collision of these forces plays out within the human soul through what we call *character,* which etymologically means markings inscribed on the soul. Despite the impersonality of these limiting powers, in the classical mythopoesis humans are nonetheless affirmed as responsible for the conduct and consequences of their life. While our character may predispose us to certain choices, and therefore consequences, the lens given by *Moira,* through which we see a distorting picture of the world, biases those choices and alters the course of our life.

Our ancestors' capacity to personify these forces enabled them to honor their power. Blessed with such images, and with the tragedies depicting their influence rippling through generations, who could not believe that life was lived on both mythological (that is, psychological) and mundane planes? Who could not respect, even tremble before, these great divinities? If destiny sweeps up wise Oedipus, or the powerful Agamemnon, what then of me?

We all still live on this mythological plane, for we are creatures of depth, not surface, whether consciousness is willing to acknowledge the invisible agencies or not. Such materialist experiments as Marxism, or rationally planned utopian communities, were doomed to failure for they sought to build a new world on the surface, without acknowledging the gods who course within each of us and through history. So, too, does religious fundamentalism insult the worth and depth of the individual, by insisting on black and white values, external authority over internal experience, and moral absolutism as a way to simplify the ambiguities of the world and the profoundly divided character we bring to it.

We can see, then, that the seemingly innocuous question, "What is my personal myth?" is of profound significance, for it is really asking, "What values, conscious or not, do I serve? What owns me? Of what am I unconscious?"

These questions cannot be answered directly, for they elude the ego's limited range of operation. But such unconscious value systems run our lives, make our choices, live their consequences, and cause the unfolding of repetitive patterns.

We can only begin to discern these mythologies through close, ongoing attention. Sober reflection on the patterns of one's life may bring hidden mythologems to the surface. Recall that by "mythologems" we mean affectively charged ideas or motifs; or clusters of motifs, and the value system and enactment which they jointly generate. This sort of reflection is intermittently possible in the first half of life, but much more so, and more necessary, in the second half.

Focused reflection requires an ego strong enough to look at personal history and willing to take responsibility for what it finds. And, obviously, one needs to have lived long enough to have created patterns. Buried in those patterns one may find operative mythologems, charged ideas which may translate as, "I need to find a wounded person for whom I can assume responsibility, having grown up with that role in my family of origin," or "I cannot get close to this person, even in marriage, because I know that in the end he/she is going to leave me, as key people have always done before."

Such charged mythologems are "ideas" of which we are largely unconscious, making them all the more powerful. In addition, they are often the flawed conclusions of real events for which we had few alternative interpretations available at the time of their occurrence. Often one is able to take the pattern, such as how one handles conflict, or the sorts of issues that recurrently arise in relationships or in self-defeating behaviors, and identify the idea behind it. The idea may make no current sense, but at the time of its origin it was the only interpretation of events.

If one learned as a child that the expression of feelings was disturbing to an anxious parent, one will likely find it difficult, even impossible, to express them later. As a result, one may be angry or depressed without being aware of the linkage which runs all the way back to childhood. If a child experienced shaming attitudes in the family of origin, he or she will likely carry a diminished sense of self into adult choices. That person, too, may be depressed while repeatedly undermining personal desires, not seeing that current life strategies are serving the old mythologem.

Recognizing these sorts of charged ideas is seldom easy. Sometimes a therapist can discern them, for he or she is outside the loop of the subjective cycle which these mythic patterns represent. When it comes to being our own therapist, the task is doubly difficult because a) we have developed a cadre of rationalizations to surround the attitude or behavior and can easily justify them to ourselves or others, and b) the challenging of these attitudes usually kicks up a measure of anxiety as one nears that place where the old wound is hiding.

Since nothing is ever lost to the psyche, all the charged experiences of our history are present, active to a greater or lesser extent, and are potentially able to usurp consciousness and repeat the original paradigm. No wonder we are creatures of habit. I have sometimes been accused of being pessimistic about growth and change. To that I would reply that it is not pessimism but realism which avers that the more we learn of these buried ideas and the energy attached to them, the more we realize the immensity of the task of rendering them conscious and of staying conscious in any given moment so as to have a possibility of a new choice.

Metaphorically, the complexity of this network of cause and effect equals the complexity of our neurological system. In the end, the psyche is logical, for it plays out over and over a reasonable response to an early experience. The idea may be an incorrect interpretation, or a lesser choice from among those later available to the adult, but it is always an idea deeply implanted in psychic life by the vicissitudes of history. Ignorance of those deeply planted ideas obliges their repetition, which in turn interferes with and thwarts the developmental motives of the Self.

Still another way to identify the implicit mythological systems within which we operate is by paying careful attention to our dreams. We do not know whence dreams come, but we do know that if we attend to them with an open sensibility they can offer a wisdom which ego may find hard to bear at times, but which will always enlarge its journey. While dreams speak a highly idiosyncratic language, our capacity to recognize in their metaphors a mythology that runs counter to that which is acted out in our daily life can help to change the course of one's personal myth. Something in us knows much more than the ego does, and in time the ego may learn to enlarge its frame to include this other wisdom. That is how one benefits from the compensatory power of the unconscious as it seeks to enlarge the narrow frame of consciousness.

Additionally, one may ask an intimate partner, who will be ever ready to tell us what is wrong with us, where we screw up, where we need to change course, what we ought to do with this journey. Sometimes they are even right.

Can we consciously, deliberately, change our myth? Well, yes and no. Some have taken on such a project in a very deliberate way. William Blake expressed the opinion that if he did not create his own myth he would then be enslaved to that of another. And William Butler Yeats created, in part out of his wife's active imagination, in part out of his own readings in theosophy, an extremely elaborate history/psychology of individual and world culture. But the mythological systems of both Blake and Yeats are so idiosyncratic, so private, that most of us need help to understand them and to decipher the role they play in their poems.

Recently, the Contemporary Arts Museum of Houston presented an exhibition of works featuring those who sought to create personal, mythological systems. Among them was a woman who wrote down everything she could remember about Shakespeare's plays. She had a good memory, but all her lists combined represented perhaps one-tenth of one per cent of what Shakespeare wrote. Someone else created a time line, little cubes which represented each day of his life or that of his culture, from the day of Kennedy's assassination through the last day of the last millennium. Still a third presented his paranoid, or not so paranoid, view of international corporate conspiracies, with lines drawn between interlocked companies and/or interest groups. What evolved was reminiscent of a mandala or rose-window.

Once again, each of these personal mythologies was rendered conscious, but represented something so idiosyncratic as to have little utility for others. Moreover, each mythic fragment was a testimony to only that small portion of psychic life which was conscious. I mean no criticism by this, either aesthetic or psychological. Rather I admire the attempt to make the invisible world conscious in some fashion, even as the byproducts remain fragmentary and the deeper gods elusive.

A far more moving personal mythology came from a man who told of returning to his birth village in eastern Poland. All of his family were murdered, along with the rest of the Jewish community of that village—all but one. One man returned from hiding and, finding the Jewish cemetery demolished and fragments of stone scattered everywhere, he took on as his life's work the recovery and reassembly of those fragments in a jigsaw puzzle which, while heart-breaking as a project, honors his community and gives him a conscious mythology.[28]

Normally, our mythologies are less dramatic, less conscious. When one undertakes the sincere survey of one's patterns, seeking the driving forces which create patterns, and when one

---

[28] This story was told to me many years ago by Milton Rokeach, who had interviewed this man personally.

watches dreams, observes the recurrence of complexes and hears the comments of therapists and friends, then one does in fact lift up and out of the unconscious world the value fabric which underlies our daily lives. Do we then approve, assent to, wish to endorse these mythologems? Can we agree that they represent our best self, or that for which we wish to stand? Are they then the challenge which consciousness must take on further, in order to lead a more ethical life, a more mature life, a more individuated journey?

As difficult as this project may be, it is the central work of the second half of life. Consider Jung's cogent remark:

> The reason why consciousness exists, and why there is an urge to widen and deepen it, is very simple: without consciousness things go less well.[29]

Of course, however conscious we are, we will continue to encounter the suffering and struggles of life, but through self-examination one may also be able, from time to time, to actually live one's own journey, not that of one's parents or one's culture, or one's trauma.

We are, inescapably, mythological beings. The only questions are: what myth and whose, ours or someone else's?

---

[29] "Analytical Psychology and 'Weltanschauung,' " *The Structure and Dynamics of the Psyche,* CW 8, par. 695.

4
What Is My Vocation?

When we reflect on the experiences of youth, our own or that of others, what grounds us in a tribal mythos, gives a sense of belonging to an historic fabric, links us to transcendent energies, provides a communal identity, initiates us into the mystery of our private journeys? Precious little, it seems.

Older cultures practiced rites of adolescent passage intended to cut the powerful tie to the family of origin, but they had no interest in personal development as we think of it today. Their priority was to overthrow, or overcome, one's childhood naiveté and immaturity in order to produce independent adults who could step into roles necessary to the survival of the tribe.

In Western culture, the concept of "the individual" has become prominent over the last four centuries as a result of the diminishment of the powers of state and church on the one hand, and the erosion of tribal mythologies on the other. As Jung put it, the modern fell off the roof of the medieval cathedral into the abyss of the Self.[30] Where once one could see the comforting anchoring architecture of mace and miter—castle and church—today one sees towers of commerce, icons of business, moving soulless abstractions between computers.

Today we tell our young to "dress for success," gain computer skills, find a partner, establish fiscal security, and someday it will all add up. It seldom does. The idea of vocation (from Latin *vocatus*, a calling or summons), what one is called to do with one's life energies, is replaced by career planning. Such advice unwittingly betrays because it trivializes our humanity. There is nothing wrong with work, quite the contrary, but to choose a

---

[30] *Letters*, vol. 2, p. 569. For further discussion of this theme, see Hollis, *Tracking the Gods: The Place of Myth in Modern Life.*

lifetime's occupation based on a paycheck or future pension is deeply destructive to the soul.

In different stages of life, our vocation evolves. As children, our calling is of course to play, to learn the ways of the world and to explore our energies, interests and talents. In the next phase of life, our vocation is to separate from our dependence on hearth and home and assume adult roles. We need to develop sufficient ego strength to hold a job, tough out difficulties, commit to relationships, accept responsibility for others, even when we may still want someone to take care of us. Whoever has not accomplished these ego tasks still has unfinished business. Another way of putting it is that the question which the first half of life asks of us is: "Do you have enough energy, courage, resourcefulness, to enter the world, take on its demands, and create your own conscious place in it?"

Notice that these tasks are obliged of us without the separating, confirming and linking rites of passage that were offered our distant ancestors. For this reason, many immature persons, unseparated from their own infantile agendas, are trying to be parents, partners, responsible employees and reliable friends. While the conditions of material life—food, health, comfort—are now readily available for most of us, it is far more difficult to become psychologically mature today than at any time in history.

In the second half of life, the questions become: "Who now, apart from the roles you play, are you? What does the soul ask of you? Do you have the wherewithal to shift course, deconstruct your painfully achieved identity, risking failure, marginalization and loss of collective approval?"

No small task.

The whole second half of life calls us to a spiritual, by which I mean psychological, agenda, while maintaining one's participation in the social community.

Over and over Jung noted that we have been forced to become psychological. From Immanuel Kant on to Werner Heisenberg and quantum physics, we have been obliged to acknowledge that our sense of reality is subjective and distorted. Our experience is simply our experience, not what may *really* have happened out there. Our ancestors could still believe in the literal reality of their tribal mythos, and be enlarged or diminished by their participation in it, but modern science has demonstrated that whatever we react to is *our* reaction, *our* meaning, *our* idiosyncratic construct. Indeed, we have been forced to become psychological because it is in the human psyche, the realm of personal experience, that we find our meaning, and as often as not a private meaning at that.

I am not saying that events do not occur extraneous to ourselves, but rather that our experience of them is both privileged and biased by our subjectivity. A growing respect for the power of the inner world is evident in our culture even though most of modern psychiatry and psychology tries to deny it. The betrayal of the ordinary person by my profession is shameful and shortsighted. It is a flight from consciousness, a narrowing of humanity, a failure of nerve before the large challenge of contemporary Western culture.

Yes, we are behaviors and cognitions and psychopharmacological processes, but add them together and one still has the mystery of identity, of vocation, of suffering, of meaning. And neither psychiatry nor psychology, as mostly practiced today, addresses any of the above. How can we not suffer a sickness of the soul when such important questions are ignored? Whatever the strengths and weaknesses of analytic psychology, at least Jung and those he influenced share a common conviction: that soul questions *matter.*

With the ever-increasing accumulation of information and the manipulation of nature, it is no surprise that we fall into the fantasy of omnipotence. Having struggled to gain ego strength, to wrest our infant selves from the sleep of instinctual longing, we have privileged consciousness, overvalued our rational powers, and thereby left ourselves open to unexpected attacks from the unconscious. The darkening dilemmas of energy overuse and environmental pollution are the results of the assertion of ego control over the primal forces of nature. The imperialism of materialism leads to personal and collective neuroses, a splitting from nature, which only ensures that nature, like the old *Nemesis*, will perforce exact revenge by irruptions and usurpations of our ego-framed world. The fragile balance between ego and nature can so easily be upset by unknown forces from below.

I believe strongly in the human will, for the will can melt mountains, or at least many of them. But one mountain it does not melt is time, which in the end will conquer us all—flesh, blood and bone.

I also affirm the power of intentionality. Some thoughtful observers have spoken of the efficacy of prayer, whether or not there is some One who is listening, as a form of intentionality which brings purpose to one's life. More and more studies suggest that healing energies are activated, for oneself and for others, as a result of prayer. Intentionality is clearly a means whereby energy can serve development. It is also a prerequisite to meaning. What I intend will be the focus of my energies.

The affirmation of intentionality reflects an existentialist perspective, a view which offers much to the appreciation of human dignity and responsibility. I am as I choose; I am what I chose. My existence is the sum of my value choices. Few would argue with that. However, a more sober view suggests that many of our choices are in fact made for us when we ignore the role of the unconscious, of the complexes, and the influence of ancestral and cultural values. As much as I admire Jean Paul Sartre and Albert Camus, and as much as I counsel accepting responsibility for our choices, I am required by experience to acknowledge the presence of dark gods in all we do.

Consider a man who at all times strives to help others. He serves on all the local committees—school boards, scout troops, fundraisers, the lot. In time he becomes indispensable to the community and he is named Citizen of the Year. No one suspects that he may have sacrificed his own individuation imperative, his vocation, his family's needs, his appointed meeting with the soul, in service to an infantile need for the approval of others. We do not judge this primal need. But it is possible that the fortuities of his fated family of origin withheld approval, and his journey was distorted and reorganized around this need. What seems selfless service to others may in fact be a deep narcissistic wound that occasioned a deadly sacrifice of his own summons to personhood. Can unblemished good come from flawed origins? Think about it.

Or think of a woman who is the "go to" person in her company. She is always courteous, efficient, productive, available for new assignments, flawless and exacting, more than competent. She is praised and promoted as an example to others. Meanwhile, her fear of criticism has created a monstrous inner critic who gives her no peace. She so fears the criticism of others that she is owned by her perfectionism, driven by an obsessive-compulsive need for approval. Of course the company loves her, exploits her, rewards her. Outside, she is a model employee; inside, she weeps in deep, lonely anguish. Why? Because she walks in shoes too small, and, alas, knows it.

In short, we know not what drives the other, just as we may not know what drives ourselves. Recall that the shadow may often be found in the midst of virtue, that even good can become demonic when it is not balanced by consciousness of its opposite.

Who among us is free of these sorts of deeply painful agendas: that we must gain the love of the other, or keep them at a distance lest they smother us, or use them to stay in control of our fragile environment? Are any of us immune to this common consequence of adapting to the demands of a powerful external world? The existentialists summon us to responsibility and choice, and I wish their arguments were still as compelling to me as they used to be. But today I am obliged to believe that they underestimate the seductiveness of the dark gods, their terrible power to insinuate themselves into our lives when we least suspect their presence. How, then, can we believe we choose, if we know not the place from which our choice emanates?

I have often thought on the meaning of the Jesus story. To me the most compelling part is not the resurrection, which may or may not have happened, or the compassion that Christ manifested, which I can believe. Rather I have always been moved by his dark night in the Garden of Gethsemane where he was so deeply divided. To go down into that city was to die a death of horror and ignominy. To flee to the desert was surely more attractive. Who among us would not take the opportunity to flee, and who would not then suffer in the desert, in that terrible freedom which took us away from our vocation? Either way brings terrible suffering. One is a suffering that authenticates one's values; one is the suffering that comes from living inauthentically. We all know this latter, for it is our common condition, even as the former is our common summons.

Nikos Kazantzakis's novel, *The Last Temptation of Christ*, is a powerful rendering of this dilemma. The greatest temptation of the Jesus the carpenter is to have an ordinary life, untroubled, comfortable, married with kids, living in the suburbs, commuting to work. How preferable to an appointment at Golgotha. The feckless cavil of the fundamentalists at Kazantzakis's novel and subsequent movie is a measure of how terrifying the encounter with one's vocation can be. The struggle he depicts in the life of Jesus is precisely what makes Christ relevant today.

The old Docetic heresy of a disembodied spirit on the planet playing a spectral drama, without real blood, real fear, real suffering, demeans the carpenter and renders his passion irrelevant to our daily lives. It is only in his choice and suffering that we see a model for our own journey. The key moment comes when Jesus says, "Not my will, but Thine." (Matt. 26:39) This is a perilous place to be, for sure, but the willingness of ego to serve the summons from the Self is what makes this story universal. To make this Jewish prophet more than human is to render him irrelevant to our common condition; to see his struggle as our struggle is to provide a paradigm for our own daily life.

How do we find our vocation? In the end, it is through the capacity of the ego to forego its need for security and comfort in service to some deeper force. But this is not easy. When does the summons come from the Self, or the Divine, and when from a complex? This difficult discernment is why the process of choice has to occur over time, with continuous review and reflection. Only in movies do great decisions come in a flash; or signal dreams change everything completely or clearly. The real choices in life will always involve the conflict between competing values, each of which has some considerable claim upon us, or there would be no difficulty in the first place.

Usually, upon close examination, the choices we face require us to leave some familiar stance in life and move into the unknown. Usually they require the acceptance of a greater level of anxiety, ambivalence and ambiguity than we find comfortable. They require us to grow, often painfully. In fact, that such choices are not easy is a good sign that we are on the right path. Even when one finally tumbles to a long-lost talent or enthusiasm, and the supportive energy is palpable, we are seldom spared old issues of diminished permission, uncertain self-worth, lack of models or obstructive fears. Those old Quislings do not go away. They hang around for a lifetime and make trouble.

In the end, the choice of vocation is also an acknowledgment that *something is in fact choosing us.* And it may have little regard for what we, the ego, wishes. It is what the gods wish that determines vocation. If we can bear that truth, and serve it, then the gods and our vocation serve us, however perilous the path. As Jung has observed, "You only feel yourself on the right road when the conflicts of duty seem to have resolved themselves, and you have become the victim of a decision made over your head."[31]

The reciprocity of energy which arises to support us when we are doing the right thing for the soul, rather than the right thing

---

[31] *Mysterium Coniunctionis,* CW 14, par. 778.

for a parental complex, is validation, even when few things in life are certain. The search for this reciprocal energy may be the contemporary form of the old Grail question, "Whom does the Grail serve?" My surmise is that the answer to the question that was so daunting to so many knights and pilgrims is, "The Grail serves those who serve it."

Thus the real Grail question is, "What am I called to serve?" The answer will play out differently for each of us, for we each have our own destiny, a separate *vocatus*. But in any case we will be served, in turn, by that which we have been summoned to serve.

5
What Are My Spiritual Points of Reference?

Quod licet Jovi, non licet bovi.
"What is good for God, is not for the cow."

This question is among the most difficult for it is the most inti-mate. Today it is fairly common to speak of sex, personal fi-nances, one's therapy and medications, one's family of origin. But talk about one's spirituality is not common. Perhaps this reluctance is an acknowledgment that spirituality is the ultimate intimacy; perhaps because the public purveyors of religiosity have so contaminated the seriousness of the question that we are reluctant to be associated with such tawdry debasement.

Yet, at the end of the day, this question is crucial. It is the essence of modernism—that is, the collective experience of the last four centuries—that the responsibility for answering this question is primarily that of the individual rather than the tribe. One may flee this responsibility through mindless descent into the diversions of popular culture, or through the bewitchment by fundamentalism of common sense and personal integrity, but the question never goes away. If it does not haunt us consciously, then it will play itself out in the superficiality, the banality, of our journey.

On the one hand we have Freud's critique of religion—which no serious person can avoid considering—describing how our in-fantile needs, fears and expectations are so easily projected onto a cosmic screen, bearing the unmistakable imprint of parental complexes. Sadly, religion is often the opiate of the people, as Marx suggested, keeping them pacified within appalling social inequities. But religion may also be a personal and cultural neuro-sis whereby the terrors of the cosmos are mediated by infan-tilizing concepts and apotropaic rituals.

65

Who can say Freud is wrong? Do we not render the world livable, horror bearable and chaos meaningful by creating fantasies of rescue, rationalizations of theological discrepancies, mantras of meaning, and then bless them with historic claims, evidence which would never hold up in court, and coercively inculcate guilt and enact ostracism for those who challenge this huddled consensus? As the old Victorian saying has it, "We are but children dear, who fret to find our bedtimes near." This is our condition: perilous, fragile and without clarity.

Whoever wishes to be honest must look, without prejudice, at how he or she may live by belief systems which have substantial measures of magical thinking, apotropaism and denial.

We all have, and we all do. Magical thinking projects the infantile fantasies of control, propitiation and external change upon the natural world or upon others. Just as we necessarily interacted with Mother and Father, so we transfer those mythologems to the cosmos. Our cries brought them to our bedside, or our compliance brought their affection and support, or our behaviors had the power to heal them, divert them, keep them near. What child has not mediated his or her terrors by such thoughts and complicit behaviors?

Similarly, apotropaisms are images or practices which ward off threatening powers: a crossed finger, a stroked rabbit's foot, a hastily repeated phrase, a knock on wood, a statuette on the car dash, an obsessive-compulsive repetitive act, and so on. These formulas and rituals are invested with the hope of withstanding and propitiating the alien powers. (One woman said to me, "Now by doing therapy I will avoid cancer, won't I?") Never mind that these stratagems fail; they may be all we have.

And, of course, denial is the most primitive of our defenses whereby we shut out what is unbearable and preserve ourselves for another day.

These archaic ideas, these defensive strategies of magical thinking, apotropaic rituals and denial, stay with us throughout our lives and contaminate our spirituality. We may feel comfortable rejecting institutional spirituality, but if we pretend to honesty and integrity, we then have to look for where these archaic ideas and defense mechanisms show up elsewhere in our lives. The point is not to judge them, but to recognize how they may still tie one to the child's world view and thereby impede maturity.[32]

I recently found myself saying essentially the same thing to three different analysands in the course of a single day. Each was suffering a substantive life crisis involving marriage or career, or understanding of life. Each was suffering the universal dilemma of Job. Twenty-six hundred years ago some gifted Hebrew poet recognized the dilemma we all encounter, namely, how our spirituality may be too small, too infantilizing and too alienating from the divine.

Job thought he had a deal. He was a good boy. He played by the rules. He was a kind, caring citizen, a good family member, and even superintended the pieties of others, so deeply committed was he to righteousness. And we all know the story. When Yahweh dumps a shitload of woe upon him, Job is of course inclined to say, as we all would, "Why me?" To which the only answer is "Why not?" Then he asks, as we all would, "What did I do wrong," to which the answer is, "Nothing."

Job even has the *chutzpah,* metaphorically speaking, to seek to subpoena God as chief witness for the defense. Naturally the Party of the First Part pays no attention to subpoenas in this barely civil suit, so Job has little recourse. The self-styled comforters trot onto the scene and remonstrate with Job, insisting he must have done something wrong, for God does not arbitrarily punish the righteous, does not, as Einstein concluded, play dice with the universe.

---

[32] To these tendencies of course, we must add our inevitable, no doubt unavoidable, anthropomorphizing of the *imago Dei,* the image of God. As Xenophanes observed twenty-six centuries ago, if lions and horses had hands, they would depict the gods as lions and horses. (See W.K.C. Guthrie, *A History of Greek Philosophy,* vol. 1, pp. 399f.)

Job, and his three comforters, whom Archibald MacLeish updated in his drama *J.B.* to a fundamentalist, a Marxist and a Freudian, share one spiritual assumption. They presume that there is a contract, a deal between us and what we call God, or between the universe and us. If we live in an historic claim that such contract exists, or are driven by magical thinking to reflexively create one, or apotropaically insist on one, then we will be dismayed when our plane goes down, our child falls ill or we are stricken by intractable depression, even while rushing toward our necessary appointments with defeat and dissolution. Especially in the Western world have we instituted the value constructs of health, material comfort, security and the idea of progress, as essential provisos in our evolving contract with the universe. Bigger, better and more secure, we believe . . . .

But it is clear that there is no contract, no deal struck between the omnipotent powers of the universe and fragile beings subject to the autonomous powers of time, tide and evanescence.

No contract. Yahweh insists that Job misunderstood and that the comforters misled. He throws out the latter with His condemnation and blesses the former for the sincerity of his struggle. Job gets it. He confesses that hitherto he had heard of the Divine, but now he has had a living encounter with the truly transcendent. In that move he has shifted from infantilizing the Parties of the First Part, and a usurpation of their autonomy, to a respectful relationship to the mystery they embody. He has moved, in other words, from a behavioral contract, a presumption that conventional piety will coerce reciprocity, to a religious experience of the absolute autonomy of the Divine.[33]

As the chief qualities of religious experience are awe and humility before the *mysterium tremendum,* Job has moved from collective consciousness to a traumatic personal *metanoia,* the

---

[33] For a psychological discourse on the Job experience, see Edward F. Edinger, *Encounter with the Self: A Jungian Commentary on William Blake's* Illustrations of the Book of Job.

painful transformation of self. Are we sure that we want to have religious experience? Are we sure we want to encounter the living psyche, which is independent of our ego control? Is not theology supposed to make one feel secure? Is not dream work meant to be cool, giving one a tip on the *Tao* of the moment, and thereby a leg up on the manipulation of life? No wonder it is easier to cling to infantilizing superstition, apotropaic formulas and magical thinking. No wonder it is easier to avoid a serious analysis rather than be shaken by an encounter with our own darkness, defeated by demonic complexes or forced to give birth to a larger frame of reference whereby the values which heretofore offered comfort and spiritual locus are left behind, forever.

Thus, I felt myself drawn, in approaching the suffering of these three quite different persons, to call upon our exemplary brother Job and recall how he was obliged to move from a pietistic deal with the universe to a truly religious experience of it. Each of the three was feeling a deep sense of betrayal, although it could not be named as such. What was feeling betrayed were the principles by which they had governed their lives, the assumptions by which they lived, and the expectations they had for reciprocity. In each case, reciprocity from the universe was not forthcoming.

What is asked of them is a new theology, so to speak, a new relationship between themselves and this whirling concatenation of molecules which is our ever so fragile home. What is asked is a new psychology, one which transcends the fantasies of ego control and brings one closer to the mystery that is our journey.

One of the major differences between analytic psychology and behavioral, cognitive and psychopharmacological therapies, is that they implicitly offer the hope of control. Control stress, control depression, control your life! Depth psychology recognizes the seductive delusion of that fantasy, and therefore speaks of the powers of the outer and inner worlds as "gods." The gods will not be mocked; they have a life, will, autonomy, of their own, and resist our efforts at control.

This metaphoric language is very off-putting to other schools of therapy. So be it. To talk of the gods is to respect the autonomy and profundity of the energies of the cosmos. As Jung has argued, it is the encounter with the numinous that is the true goal of therapy. So, not adaptation, not happiness, not statistical normality, but encounter with the numinous. In such encounters we are restored to our proper place in the larger order. Our journeys are reframed and repositioned. Awe and humility—the twin attitudes necessary for religious or psychological truth—bring new life to each of us, if we can bear them.

When I was a youth I expressed a reluctance to attend church. It was explained to me, rather forcefully, that only through corporate observance could religion really be validated. My hesitation at that time was based on two points. First, I saw a great discrepancy between the professed values—those espoused and modeled by Jesus, for example—and the models lived out on the street and in home life. I was in a segregated church, for one thing. Those of other color would not have been overtly turned away at the door, but they would quickly have known they were not welcome, without even hearing the racist attitudes I heard on a daily basis behind the scenes.

Secondly, while I had no little admiration for the inclusive attitudes and practices of Jesus, I had profound doubts about the miracles and implications of many Biblical admonitions as they were translated into the dogma and practice of daily life. For reasons I could not explain, the whole thing just did not feel right.

Part of what did not feel right was the all or nothing, either/or character of communal expectations. Additionally, it was exclusionary rather than inclusive, not only of people but of wider religious traditions and insights. Yet when I raised my timid objections, I was told that I simply did not understand, that the group was more important than the individual, that I would understand some day. I left then, somewhere around ten or twelve, though my body hung in until eighteen. I mean no disparagement of good people with benign intentions, but to this day I remain scarred by their denigration of my instinctual reservations and honest questions. And I have seen many in therapy who are even more deeply scarred than I. It is no small task to recover a religious attitude when the whole range of inquiry has been contaminated by the shadow problems of fear and power.

However, the questions I raised as a child were of such importance that after college I found myself in theology school, still seeking answers. During that time I was exposed to a wonderfully rich tradition of spiritual experience, speculation and even doubt —all of which I continue to draw upon. Yet, I also knew that my personal path would have to be *extra ecclesium*, outside the Church, and that I could not will it otherwise however much I so desired.

There were some notable religious writers, to whom I am still grateful, who supported my personal journey. From Paul Tillich I learned that one is "religious" not because of a set of particular beliefs but by the character of one's questions. One's religiosity will be found less as a product of the ego's convictions than of one's lived concern for ultimacy. From Tillich I learned that I *was* religious, even though I could not fit into any religious body or tradition. For a youth who suffered from guilt and ostracism, such reframing of the issue was healing.

From Dietrich Bonhoeffer I learned that one is summoned to service of some kind regardless of one's metaphysical underpinning. Before he was murdered at *K-Z Lager Flossenburg* for his opposition to Hitler, Bonhoeffer averred that the word "God" should be avoided for a century, so encrusted was it with conventional associations. This is a man, I realized, who was willing to stand, as Søren Kierkegaard defined religious experience, in absolute relationship to the absolute. Kierkegaard taught me how easy it was to confuse the blandishments of our cultural comforts, to be seduced by our ethical systems, and yet be terrified to stand in authentic relationship to the Absolute Other.

Each of them, in short, argued for the primacy of personal experience, for a summons to the large, for spiritual integrity rather than magical thinking and special deals.

Later, it was the work of C.G. Jung that most opened for me the way in which being a person of conscientious religious character also requires one to have some deep relationship to one's personal psychological reality. Influenced by Kant as he was, Jung understood that what is not experienced is not real, and, conversely, what is real is experiential. It may or may not have its origins outside our psyche, but it will nonetheless have to be a psychic reality for it to have a personal claim on us.

No small part of the coercive hysteria of the fundamentalist agenda is based on the fact that their dogmas not only serve as anxiety disorder treatment plans and culturally infantilizing moral systems, but also betray the secret that their convictions are not truly psychologically real for them either. The hysteria of certainty is in direct proportion to uncertainty in the unconscious. Rather than embrace uncertainty as a worthy religious attitude, one which respects the Divine as other than an artifact of consciousness, the fundamentalist is obliged to crush uncertainty. Personal fear is rationalized, finessed, by assaulting the doubt of others.

No matter how pious the rhetoric, much harm is done when the integrity of one's personal experience is violated on behalf of the group's neurosis. Damage is done to those who are denied permission to take a journey of personal discovery. Many institutions have deemed the collective to be more important than the individual, fearing schism, psychosis, anarchy. But such institutions, no matter now noble their intent, do great harm. In service to fear, they sabotage the private journey which is the obligation of all, and thereby deny the power of the gods to find expression through each of us. This is bad theology and bad psychology. It does violence to the soul and is the ultimate impiety. It represents, in the end, the defense against a genuine religious encounter.

The second characteristic, the summons to the large, asks that our timorous ego step out from behind its fear and grow as large as our journey requires. We have heard Jung say we live in shoes too small, but we need to recall his powerful challenge:

> The spirit of evil is fear, negation, the adversary who opposes life in its struggle for eternal duration and thwarts every great deed, who infuses into the body the poison of weakness and age through the treacherous bite of the serpent; he is the spirit of regression, who threatens us with bondage to the mother and with dissolution and extinction in the unconscious. For the hero, fear is a challenge and a task, because only boldness can deliver from fear. And if the risk is not taken, the meaning of life is somehow violated, and the whole future is condemned to hopeless staleness, to a drab grey lit only by will-o'-the-wisps.[34]

This passage bears further contemplation.

Evil is what thwarts life, what blocks its purpose, intention, teleology. And the source of this evil is inescapable, per se, for fear is ubiquitous. It is the bedrock of our common condition.

Again, we hear life say to each of us, from early days, "The world is big and you are small. Now, deal with that." Our vulnerability, our powerlessness, may be mediated somewhat by supportive family and tribal mythos, or not, as the case may be, but ultimately the world will break through our delusions and remind us of our powerlessness. Fear, then, is the enemy. Whenever fear is not made conscious, chances are very strong that the theology, the psychology, the politics will be fear-driven, fear-based, fear-compensating. From such origins much evil will arise, for, as we have seen, even our most reasoned choices may serve something sinister.

When Jung speaks of regression, he reminds us of that daily struggle between progression and regression, the slippery slide, the desire to fall back into the mother. By "mother" here, we mean not the personal mother, but the source, the origin, the all-comforting, protective, nurturant other who offers freedom from the pain which consciousness occasions. The Edenic Tree

---

[34] *Symbols of Transformatioin,* CW 5, par. 551.

of Life nurtures; the Tree of Knowledge exiles, forever. Jung is not suggesting that one be impervious to regression, nor able to avoid it wholly, but when the spirit of regression prevails we are living a diminished life and any larger purpose is obviated.

What Jung calls the hero in the above passage is that specific energy which the Self provides to mobilize libido in the service of development. The hero is that archetypally charged structure which confronts the fear and the sundry seductions of the deep on a daily basis. Recall the perils of Odysseus and his crew, and the many temptations they experienced along the way, offering surcease from the perilous rigors of the wine-dark sea.

We have a tendency to use our partners as our source of surcease. To drown in the arms of the beloved is thought to be desirable, the be-all and end-all of love; indeed, it is the chief fantasy of popular culture. We make of our institutions surrogate mothers to care for us, to keep us safe and sheltered, to help us avoid growing up. Who wants to be out on the frosty heath, the foam-flecked waves, the edge of the abyss? Who does not desire the innocent sleep of childhood, the sweet bondage of the void?

If we are not bold, if we refuse risk, then we violate the *telos* of our life. In truth, we violate this transcendent purpose much of the time. Yet something deep within impels us forward, ever renewing the possibility of the incarnation of meaning through the gift of individual expression.

Following the passage quoted above, Jung writes:

> The natural course of life demands that the young person should sacrifice his childhood and his childish dependence on the physical parents, lest he remain caught body and soul in the bonds of unconscious incest. This regressive tendency has been consistently opposed from the most primitive times by the great psychotherapeutic systems which we know as the religions. They seek to create an autonomous consciousness by weaning mankind away from the sleep of childhood.[35]

---

[35] Ibid., par. 553.

By "psychotherapeutic systems" Jung means the tribal *mythos,* those charged imagos which mobilize libido in service to the development of adulthood and community. Such archetypal symbols operate as transformers. They convert psychic energy to form, pattern, direction. We often call these shaping patterns instincts, and so they are. The need for meaning, for transcendent connection, is as deeply instinctual as hunger or sexuality. Remove those imagos progressively discharging energy and the child will remain at home, protected, dependent, regressed.

Such a state of symbolic decay is the central dilemma of the modern era. Tribal imagos are enervated if not altogether absent. Contrived values such as financial security, hedonism and self-absorption are the norm. No wonder we are so neurotic, addicted, rootless, adrift. Millions abandon the worth of their journey to the search for more and better material goods. Millions of others seek the restoration of the old time religion, a futile infusion of new wine into old wineskins. Others find in this crisis of meaning a personal challenge.

The third value, the affirmation of spiritual integrity, is all the more difficult given the spiritual desolation of the present.

In the face of our fear, we all search for magic: the right theology, the right psychology, the right diet, right mantra, right partner—whatever offers to hold back the night. The desire for magic reflects our desire for instant transformation, for rescue and protection. It is the fantasy of the primitive mind which lurks beneath the veneer of our civilized selves. We cannot help but desire magic. Yet, sooner or later, we are challenged to leave magic behind and open ourselves to the universe in all its wonder and terror. Sooner or later we must face the summons to grow up. And if we do, we still must do so again each day, for the fear which haunts our condition renews itself with every dawn.

Spiritual integrity obliges each of us to value the primacy of personal experience, for that is how the divinities come to us. If it does not feel right for us within, then it isn't. We may contort our behavior, deny our feelings, seek to adjust to communal expectations, but in the end it will never quite work. As children most of us knew that, but we were outvoted, powerless then to create our own lives, obliged to adapt outwardly and go underground inwardly. The legacy of that power inequity abides, and too often we spend our lives in quiet adaptation and silent, angry or despairing dissent.

On one occasion I visited my father at his church in a retirement center. The service was buoyant and cheerful, yet felt altogether phony to me. The gaiety and good cheer were well intended but seemed overkill, a form of denial. Outside in the parking lot, my father turned to me and said, not knowing what my private thoughts had been, "We are all just here studying for our final exams." He smiled knowingly, with a twinkle and a hint of irony. I was deeply relieved that he knew, and that he was telling me he knew. At that moment there was spiritual integrity between us. We were co-conspirators in secret honesty.

Spiritual integrity means that we learn to be honest with ourselves. Coming close to that place, one alerts the anxious, ever-vigilant complexes which seek to protect us from even larger anxiety. These sentinels shut down feeling, divert thought, collude in collectivity. To override the defense system is not an easy task. But when we can, we see that we do have a strong instinct which tells us what is right for us.

In dreams and fairy tales, this guiding instinct might be embodied in the image of a dog whose capacity to hear what is below the level of hearing, see what is invisible, sniff what is off-stage, represents the inner directedness we all possess. Such a capacity of knowing is present to every organism, serving its survival and well-being. But at some time in the past, acting on that instinct became sufficiently costly that we learned to shut it down, thereby colluding against ourselves. Approaching this risky zone is enough to make the rantings of the demagogues effective in suborning spiritual hypocrisy. To know what is true for us, to feel what we really feel, to believe what makes sense of our unique journey—this is the essence of living a life of spiritual integrity. Not easy, not common.

In an earlier book, *Tracking the Gods,* I identified three characteristics of spiritual experience which bear repeating here. They are 1) the principle of resonance; 2) the encounter with the numinous; and 3) the engagement in depth.

The principle of resonance (re-sounding) suggests that if something is right for us, consonant with our soul's need, it will set off an inner tuning fork. The hum of resonance means that some image, belief or practice is right for us because something within us responds. Like responds to like. Clearly ego cannot cause this to happen; resonance is autonomous, an expression of the Self. We may try to will something to be true, but it will never be true *to* us unless it is true *for* us.

As we pick through the debris of the spiritual traditions, we may find many images that still carry a charge of energy. The specific images will of course vary from person to person, but our task is to assemble the bits and pieces together in a personally coherent form supportive of the psyche's intent. This mythological cloak made of motley is our individual attire. For very few will an entire suit be transferable from one to another. Having someone else's experience is an unlikely occurrence, although corporate religions often act as if such were the norm. This is like expecting all of us to fall in love with the same person in the same way, and even that is more likely than our having the same religious experience.

The principle of resonance is thus the private means by which a person may know what works. And no one else has the right to predetermine that person's experience. Evangelical fervor is an imperialist compensation for unconscious doubt, and represents a potential wound to the spiritual integrity of others.

Secondly, the encounter with the numinous may be the experience of daily life when one has become sensitized to the movement of the soul. When, in the Gnostic Gospel of Thomas, Jesus says that the kingdom of God is spread all over the world and we do not see it, he is suggesting that the numinous is omnipresent. When William Blake saw eternity in a grain of sand and in the transient flower, he was experiencing the numinosity of everyday life, the macrocosm in the microcosm.

The word "numinous" comes from the Latin *numen,* which means to nod or beckon. Thus, autonomous energy nods, beckons, summons the attention. This energy needs us, as Rilke argues in his ninth *Duino Elegy,* to bring it to consciousness. And when the artist Paul Eluard suggested that there is another world and it is *this* one, he and the other surrealists were calling attention to the presence of the invisible world in the midst of the visible. We have, as we all know, achieved stunning control over the material world. But at the same time we have lost almost all sense of the presence of the invisible one. Nonetheless, that world is there, active, summoning, nodding to those willing to own their experience and reflect with honesty on the encounter.

Lastly, the engagement in depth means that we are asked to be larger, to be big folks rather than frightened children. It is one thing to have a scared kid within, as we all do; it is something else to turn the conduct of our life over to that child. A therapist friend of mine once said she could tell in the first hour whether the person who came to her was a big kid or a little kid. The former were willing to grow up, take responsibility for themselves, often painfully, and the latter were still looking for mommy and daddy to make the hurt go away. Serious analysis or therapy depends upon the emergence of the former, as does a serious life.

Engagement with depth requires us to recognize that our contracts with the universe, our slick deals, our rationalizations, do not exist, made null and void by the autonomy of the world. We are asked to experience the profundity of that mystery which both courses through us and animates the world around. This engagement brings meaning and beauty to our lives. It may sometimes bring terror too, which nevertheless furthers the individuation process whereby we serve the gods by becoming more of what they intended. I have often been told by survivors of the most appalling accidents or circumstances that on reflection they would not have had it any other way, for their subsequent experience made them who they are.

Accordingly, the question, "What are my spiritual points of reference?" may only be answered in individual ways. My experience is my experience, not yours. What is yours?

Our souls long for transcendence, for meaning, for connection. This is who we most deeply are. When that need is intimidated by fear, diverted by cultural idols, or projected onto others, something terrible happens to our souls. When we learn to face our fear, open to the universe without defense and follow what beckons, we will find our true spiritual path.

The image of the Grail once symbolized such a quest. In that medieval legend the knights were directed to a place in the forest where there was no path lest they follow someone else's. While the image of the Grail no longer speaks to most of us, the evocation of that which we seek, and which seeks us, is still the most compelling of our realities. Sorting through the chaff, standing up to fear and intimidation by others, and tracking the gods in the detritus of daily life, that is what makes our journey divine. Jung reminds us that "it is not a question of belief but of experience."[36] Are we large enough to honor and act upon the reality of our experience? As Jung so eloquently adds:

> No one can know what the ultimate things are. We must therefore take them as we experience them. And if such experience helps to make life healthier, more beautiful, more complete and more satisfactory to yourself and to those you love, you may safely say: 'This was the grace of God.'[37]

---

[36] "Psychology and Religion," *Psychology and Religion,* CW 11, par. 167.
[37] Ibid.

6
What Fiction Shall Be My Truth?

> When the play, it may be the tragedy, of life is over, the
> spectator goes his way. It was a kind of fiction, a work
> of the imagination only.
> —Henry David Thoreau, *Walden.*

When we consider the lives of others, we are often amazed at the values, conscious or unconscious, personal or cultural, by which they live. When we consider that dozens of members of the royal retinue of Egypt's pharaohs were ritually garroted and laid to rest with their Lord, seemingly cooperating without protest, we are amazed. How could they? Did they not value the worth of individual life as we do? Yet those persons may be envied, for they lived within an organizing set of images that gave them a sense of spiritual locus, a social fabric which embraced them, and the promise of a continued existence in the world beyond death.

When we learn of people accepting their fated class, or role, or defined identity with equanimity, we may protest from our personal viewpoint. When we witness heroic but hopeless action in literature, like the Celtic Cuchulain wading out to sea, we often fail to grasp the meaning. We label the belief systems of our ancestors as superstitions, condescendingly judging their naiveté. Yet, if we are honest, we may be dismayed to perceive those beliefs and practices we were so sure of at one point in our life and have since outgrown. *Truth* is what we believe at the moment, and *fiction* someone else's, and lesser, belief. We all practice a reverse irredentism—we wish to disown quickly what we once owned, or what owned us.

The tests of truth have varied from era to era. For the moment, truth may loosely be defined as that which is confirmed by our experience, but often what that experience was, really, is deceptive and subject to revision over time. Truth is often defined through consensual reality; that is, what most people believe. But we have seen groups possessed by hysterical outbreaks and prey to psychic contagions. They have believed their neighbors to be the source of a plague, say, and, with the blessings of sacred institutions, persecuted them. They have been possessed by fads, fashions, collective projections, collective denial. They have believed the gods blessed their dirty work, as we see so clearly in Joseph Conrad's *Heart of Darkness*, for example.

Truth has also been defined by external authority, a ruler or institution, whose priesthood may be deluded, gripped by a complex, or simply ignorant according to the subsequent judgment of history. My grandfather, in a jocular moment, told me his navel was where an Indian shot him with an arrow. Despite the fact that I had a similar "wound" and no recollection of an arrow, my belief in his veracity was unshaken for many years, so great was his moral authority to a child.

Truth may also be defined, as it was by the American pragmatists at the end of the nineteenth century—Josiah Royce, Charles S. Pierce, John Dewey, William James—as the practical outcome of an idea, its utility a result of volition. Or truth may be prepositional, defined by its own terms: let X equal Y, etc. Truth may be empirical, tested and confirmed by the weight of our senses, even though our senses often deceive. As the Nobel physicist Werner Heisenberg noted, we cannot observe an object without changing it, cannot fix it in both time and space, and therefore we participate in self-delusion when we believe we truly weigh, measure, manipulate.

We have seen earlier in the examination of personal myth that what we think is true is often the expression of the complex which owns us at the moment. I believe I am in love, that the beloved is as I perceive him or her to be, and that this experience is indisputable and self-defining. In another mood state, the beloved is wholly altered, even despised. What then was or is true? At the moment of exalted feeling, one is prepared to swear allegiance forever; in a later moment, the other may be, alien, incomprehensible. What was true was a psychic construct whose prevailing power was transient.

Since Kant we have been forced to take account of our psychological realities: our subjective reading of the world, our tendency to privilege that subjective reality over the radical otherness of the external world, and the fact that certain mechanisms, such as repression, projection, displacement, splitting, etc., are often if not always at work in our perceptions. Jung was a post-Kantian, of course, and noted that, paradoxically, even when consensual reality was offended by one person's construct, that construct constituted the psychological reality of that person. Of a woman who believed she had been on the moon, he said she had *really* been on the moon. Her experience was true for her, and respect for such reality, without collusion in it, is incumbent upon the therapist.

We may label another person's experience a delusion, hallucination or mistaken. Yet it is their reality. I once knew a woman who believed that her long-lost fighter pilot lover flew in her hospital room to communicate his love. As the hospital was not far from an airport, planes frequently flew over. She importuned others as to whether they heard or saw a plane and, when they said they did, she felt confirmed in her belief. Though he was killed at the end of the war, can we say that he was dead to this woman, that he did not remain present to her? Can we say that love does not survive death? Can we say that the dead do not travel with us still? Death does not end a life any more than divorce ends a marriage.

So we live, then, according to the fictions which hold sway over us. No matter their origin—external authority, tradition, family of origin, popular culture—fictions hold sway over us and constitute our truth. In his poem "Sunday Morning," Wallace Stevens depicts a circle of solar celebrants, worshipping the sun, "Not as a god, but as a god might be, / Naked among them, like a savage source."[38]

Only a modern could have written those lines, someone who has fallen out of the direct apprehension of divinity, but who understands full well the necessity of metaphor in approaching the unapproachable. The words "might be," and "like" testify to an awareness of image, that is, a conscious fiction, in order to apprehend and communicate experience.

Such conscious use of image is the essence of sanity. To be bewitched by literalism, to fall in love with our own constructs, is a form of insanity. It is the oldest of religious sins, committed everywhere by the literalist inside each of us—the sin of idolatry. Only consciousness of fiction can spare us from literalism. Literalism manifests when a psychotic patient sees the sun as a devouring monster, for example, rather than a powerful symbol of something devouring in that person's life at that time.

Such literalism bewitches fundamentalists of all stripes when they seek refuge within the limits of their images rather than recalling that a sacred image points beyond itself toward the invisible. Just as we would not use a CAT-scan to search for the anima or the shadow, we should not cling to the tribal experience of another time and place.

The word "fiction" comes from the Latin *facere*, to make or fabricate (a factory in English is a *Fabrik* in German). Similarly, the word "poetry" comes from the Greek *poiein,* which also means to make. This capacity for making, this constitutive agency, is our greatest power. It makes meaning, and the communication of that meaning, possible.

Thus, the question, "What fiction shall be my truth?" is a very large challenge to modern consciousness. Tribal mythologies and sacred institutions have lost their numinosity for most of us. So the responsibility for myth has fallen upon the individual. Either we create our myths, our fictions, as Blake said, or we

---

[38] In Richard Ellmann and Robert O'Clair, eds., *Modern Poems: An Introduction to Poetry,* p. 94.

will be enslaved to someone else's.

Søren Kierkegaard describes the fiction by which Socrates lived his soul's journey:

> Socrates could not prove the immortality of the soul: He simply said: This matter occupies me so much that I will order my life as though immortality were a fact—should there be none, *eh bien.* I still do not regret my choice; for this is the only thing that concerns me.[39]

According to Kierkegaard, Socrates was spared the trap of bewitchment by his fictions, spared seduction by his constructs. His wisdom lay, by report of the Oracle of Apollo at Delphi, in the fact that he knew that he did not know. His life was a search for constructs which gave meaning and purpose to his existence. He served a worthy fiction, not whether or not immortality exists, but that the idea of immortality is worth a lifetime's devotion.

What about us? What have we found to give worth to our own journey? What fictions do we serve? I have concluded that, metaphorically, I live my life in service to Hermes. This may seem a preposterous thing to say. But Hermes is the god of the in-between, the messenger, the shadowy presence who slips across boundaries. As a teacher, a writer, an analyst, I spend my life in the in-between: between subject matter and student, thesis and reader, unconscious and analysand. I did not choose this life; it chose me. As of this hour it continues to choose me.

To say that I serve a god is to evoke the position of Wallace Stevens, the conscious user of fiction. To say that I serve Hermes is to say that what we call a god, that personified energy which moves the cosmos, drives history, has taken me. That I can name the god and choose to honor it is to be conscious rather than enslaved. Whenever we can use such fictions consciously, then we can remain awake on our journey, rather than being put to sleep by literalism or naiveté.

---

[39] *Papers and Journals: A Selection,* p. 503.

A worthy fiction leads one to a worthy life. What fiction, then, is your truth right now, your guiding image? Is it worthy of the high summons of a life's journey? Is it possible that your fiction has been outlived? What is its source—mom and dad, culture, trauma? Do you like what you find? Are you choosing or being chosen? By what fiction does your life fulfill its truth, betray its truth, avoid its truth?

To find our truths we must travel consciously, by way of our fictions.

7
What Is My Obligation to the World?

Summer lightning says
It doesn't matter
If the instant accident
That arcs the gap between two bodies
Is aware of loneliness or love.
— Robert Ely, "Affinities."

There is a paradox at the heart of all relationships. We cannot know ourselves without the dialectical encounter with others, an encounter which obliges us to define who we are, and then to grow by incorporating our experience of the other. Yet, we cannot find any relationship more evolved than the level of development we bring to it. As always, truth is paradoxical. Holding the tension of these opposites is key to the question of what we owe the world. Such a relationship, and responsibility to self and world, is a constantly shifting line, and we are never free of the need to discern where that line is.

Too often people have heard Jung's idea of individuation as a summons to self-interest only, even to narcissism. Nothing could be further from the truth. As Jung notes:

> The unrelated human being lacks wholeness, for he can achieve wholeness only through the soul, and the soul cannot exist without its other side, which is always found in a "You." Wholeness is a combination of I and You and these show themselves to be parts of a transcendent unity whose nature can only be grasped symbolically.[40]

This observation bears some analysis for it is not as transparent as it may seem at first glance. What Jung is really emphasizing is the dialectic, the necessary tension of opposites, which by definition require an I and a not-I. Without the other, one

---

[40] "The Psychology of the Transference," *The Practice of Psychotherapy,* CW 16, par. 454.

remains caught in the limited narcissistic loop whereby one's sense of reality is secure and unchallenged by other possibilities. Many times we choose to remain uninformed, unchallenged, safe in a self-referential world. Ignorance, xenophobia, bigotry and stultification feed on such self-referential psychology.

Engaging the not-I may cause anxiety, but it is also the catalyst for growth and consciousness. One could say that consciousness is born, and the individual launched, the moment the infant first realizes that it is no longer synonymous with its mother. This trauma of separation begets a longing to return to the security of that initial bond, even though this regressive impulse is the enemy of life.[41] The You, the opposite, obliges enlargement to contain this not-I and thus is the requisite for growth. But, as Jung says, wholeness obliges that we account for the opposites.

One can see how Jung's observation may fuel the romantic fantasy of togetherness, merging with the other. To lie in the arms of the other, *le petite morte* of sexuality, is, after all, to die. And dying is so attractive because the pain of the opposites is so great. This fantasy of the other in whom we can submerge ourselves and return to the source is the chief fuel of regressive behaviors, whether they be romantic fantasies, drug addiction or over-identification with a group or ideology. What is not clear here, but which Jung argues elsewhere, is that the other must also be found in oneself.

Finding the other in oneself involves a dialogue which may impede or improve the quality of relatedness to the outer other. Our romantic ideologies seek the other for completion and wholeness, and yet at the same time carry the seeds of annihilation. Failing to find the other in ourselves, to experience our own unfolding mystery, our quirks, our shadow, our complexes, neuroses and aspirations, is to fail to find the most interesting relationship of all. We always remain a mystery to ourselves, so

---

[41] See Hollis, *The Eden Project: In Search of the Magical Other,* for a fuller discussion of this tension.

we have a life-long agenda for growth and development. Whoever is bored has not yet awakened to the large drama that courses within.

A narcissistic loop, where only ideas familiar to the ego are acceptable, is a prescription for torpor. A preoccupation with merging with the other can lead to annihilation. Conversely, the tension between self and other furthers individuation.

There is an activity of the Self that assists in this engagement, this *Auseinandersetzung* ("coming to terms with"). Jung calls it the transcendent function. It is a manifestation of the Self's search for wholeness, for reconciling opposites. An example might be a dream we recall upon waking. By definition, we cannot know what is in the unconscious, but we do know that the conscious world did not manufacture the dream. Accordingly, the dream images hover in a mid-point between the unconscious and consciousness. By attending to them, we may further the relationship between the two worlds which are yet one.

Similarly, symptomology, from a depth psychological perspective, is a manifestation of the meeting point between conscious and unconscious life through affect, soma or behavior. Therapy may be understood then as a focus on such meeting points so as to discern the intentionality of the psyche and to mobilize consciousness in support. Such mutuality of intent, between Self and ego, promotes healing and well-being, whether or not the attitude is supported by the environment. As Jung notes,

> Once the unconscious content has been given form and the meaning of the formulation is understood, the question arises as to how the ego will relate to this position, and how the ego and the unconscious are to come to terms. This is the second and more important stage of the procedure, the bringing together of opposites for the production of the third: the transcendent function. At this stage it is no longer the unconscious that takes the lead, but the ego.[42]

---

[42] "The Transcendent Function," *The Structure and Dynamics of the Psyche,* CW 8, par. 181.

The depth of our journey will be found in this dialectical exchange with oneself. The role of the unconscious is to provide correctives or compensation that serve to enlarge a person. It is the role of the ego to understand and assist this agenda through the world of conscious and ethical choice. As Jung suggests,

> From the activity of the unconscious there now emerges a new content, constellated by thesis and antithesis in equal measure and standing in a *compensatory* relation to both. It thus forms the middle ground on which the opposites can be united.[43]

Out of this dialogue the stuck places can be transcended and life may flow forward in its developmental agenda.

To recognize and profoundly feel the presence of such a compensatory function, to know that it is not pathological even when symptomatic, is to stand in a deepened relationship to the soul. From where do our dreams emanate? We do not know, but they surely are present, manifesting a wisdom that enlarges consciousness. Anyone who has truly grasped this fact, internalized it, felt it, is never wholly alone again. That person participates in a transcendent relationship which changes the quality of one's journey forever. Such an individual has relationship, relationship which opens to more conscious possibilities in the dialogue with another, as well as an abiding sense of participation in mystery.

The person who has experienced primal relationships as invasive is likely to feel great need for distance in later relationships. An early sense of abandonment often manifests later as neediness, especially for reassurance. One will stay a prisoner of these templates until corrected or enlarged by other experiences. Thus the dialogue with others, and with oneself, are absolutely essential to the transcendence of one's early fate.

The meeting place of such opposites is generally attended by symbol, for only symbol can encompass the opposites which ego cannot embrace on its own. Thus, when cultures describe their

---

[43] "Definitions," *Psychological Types,* CW 6, par. 825.

relationship to the gods as to parents—the Sky Father or Earth Mother, for example—they are utilizing the intermediate image, the parent, to intimate certain qualities or aspirations they experience in regard to that which is wholly other, transcendent to consciousness, and a mystery. To use such an image is not to say the deity *is* a parent; that would be naive literalism. Rather it is to say that qualities of the parent-child relationship are useful in talking about the impact such a relationship undeniably has upon one's psyche.

The transcendent third which arises out of any relationship, be it a dream image, romance, or encounter with the gods, serves to embody the opposites; it points in both directions and holds affect until it can be transformed into experience. Genuine relationship, in whatever forum, is a mystery: an encounter between self and other, whether that other is external or internal. Such mystery, far from being regressive—as is our desire to lose ourselves in an other—is invariably enlarging because one is obliged to grow in order to contain the experience of the opposites. Quite contrary to the fantasy of romance, one should beware of what one asks for; relationship will oblige growth not regression, complexity not simplicity, and involve coming to terms with the tension of opposites which each party embodies.

Thus, obliquely, we come back to the question this chapter addresses: "What is my obligation to the world?" As one may have guessed by now, there is always, at all times, a dual obligation. An obligation to the world is sometimes overprogrammed in the child's early experience. In such contexts, one will be caught in a template which compels ready response to the world, at the cost of neglecting the Self's intent. The greater the outer adaptation required, the harder will it be for such a person to have a relationship with the Self.

Much of adult life is conditioned by overgeneralizations of early experience. It is not that one is incapable of alternative choices, but rather that the relational model of self and world is automatically inclined to the familiar. Thus a person may have inordinate difficulty in acknowledging and acting upon the legitimate imperatives of the soul.

So, what does one owe to the world? My own answer is: respect, ethical behavior and the gift of one's own best self. We serve others by becoming ourselves, what the gods intended. As Jung has put it,

> Individuation cuts one off from personal conformity and hence from collectivity. That is the guilt which the individuant leaves behind him for the world, that is the guilt which he must endeavor to redeem. He must offer a ransom in place of himself, that is, he must bring forth values which are an equivalent substitute for his absence in the collective personal sphere.[44]

And elsewhere:

> Individuation does not shut one out from the world, but gathers the world to itself.[45]

All our social conditioning tends to foster conformity, for thereby one is most likely to have one's needs met, find security, even love. But with every adaptation there is a concomitant risk that the soul will be violated. As the Self always reacts to its violation, we may suffer depression, loss of libido for an assigned task, or recurrent nightmares. Thus a person will be driven to pay attention to a new agenda, one that may in fact seem ill-advised in the eyes of others. When Jung speaks of guilt he may really mean anxiety, the anxiety that comes from risking one's security. But in compensation, we bring our larger selves back to the world.

The evolution of the cosmos depends on the individuation of each of us. This is a very high destiny, interfered with by fate and daily compromises. It is also an imperative whose magnitude may intimidate. What we are given when we withdraw from

---

[44] "The Symbolic Life," *The Symbolic Life,* CW 18, par. 1095.
[45] "On the Nature of the Psyche," *The Practice of Psychotherapy,* CW 16, par. 432.

compromise is an opportunity for the transformation of energy into something wholly unique: the individual.

None of us can achieve wholeness, as such, for that is an imperative larger than our finite capacity. Jung believed that Jesus, the Christ for the West, and Gautama, the Buddha for the East, served as cultural imagos for the ideal of wholeness. But our wholeness is not achieved by imitating them. They traveled their journey; our own is different. Whenever we take steps to respond to the Self, whenever the ego can surrender to the Self and serve its larger perspective, we are moving toward wholeness. If the gods, or the Self, have so ordained, who then are we to flee? We are often intimidated by fear, of course, but it may be a much more fearful thing not to have been who we were meant to be than to face the fears that stand in our way.

What we owe the world, then, is respect for each person's summons to be unique. We owe ethical behavior so that we may live in a society which supports each person's possibilities. And we owe the world the contribution of our best selves. It is in our uniqueness, our special talent or capacity or calling, that we add to the richness of the world. As Gerard Manley Hopkins described, from the deep well of Being comes "all things counter, original, spare, strange."[46]

This humble achievement of unique personhood, with all its perverse permutations, is an act of the greatest praise, and what we most owe the world.

---

[46] "Pied Beauty," in Ellmann and O'Clair, eds., *Modern Poems,* p. 23.

8
"So, Ahem . . . What's This Death Business?"

> We move between two darknesses. The two entities who
> might enlighten us, the baby and the corpse, cannot do so.
> —E.M. Forster.

Thought you'd never ask. About death, that is.

Ahem . . . . Well, beats me . . . .

Most of us read the newspaper, have been around for a few
decades, know the statistics, and still act surprised by mortality.
All it takes is a loved one going down, an elevated PSA count or
a lump in the breast, and . . . ahem. Reminds me of e.e. cum-
mings's ironic choice of Buffalo Bill as a personification of vi-
tality, adventure, flash, shazam, immortality, and, as an American, no doubt granted special exemption from mortal limits:

Buffalo Bill's
defunct
   who used to
   ride a watersmooth-silver
          stallion
and break onetwothreefourfive pigeonsjustlikethat
                    Jesus
he was a handsome man
        and what I want to know is
how do you like your blueeyed boy
   Mister Death[47]

So, even a guy who seemed to transcend the ordinary proves
another citizen of the democracy of death. The real Buffalo Bill
died of uremic poisoning; no flash, no shazam—simply rusty
pipes. As Martin Heidegger pointed out, we are "Beings-toward-

---

[47] "Buffalo Bill's Defunct," in Thomas E. Foster and Elizabeth C. Guthrie,
eds., *A Year in Poetry*, p. 14.

Death,"[48] that is, time-bound creatures whose fate is extinction, propelled toward dissolution from birth, dying in every moment.

We know that any instant may bring us to the edge of the abyss, and over. Tolstoy's novella, "The Death of Ivan Ilyich," is but one example of an ordinary person finding ordinary death extraordinary. Illustrating the five typical stages described by Elisabeth Kübler-Ross in *Living with Death and Dying*, Ilyich goes through denial, anger, bargaining, depression and finally acceptance. What is so extraordinary about Tolstoy's narrative is how ordinary the experience is. But why else would he feel compelled to write such a story unless his culture, like ours, lived in the denial of death? Moreover, our culture has far surpassed nineteenth-century Russia in denial. Can anything be more neurotic than denying our own nature and spending billions on surgery, vitamins pills, hair transplants and cryogenetics to hold back "the enemy"? In the Western world, good health is well on its way to supplanting materialism as the new religion.

Recently I heard a discussion on the subject of the Black Madonna, a growing fascination with which no doubt reflects an effort to compensate the one-sided image of the bloodless, ethereal Virgin Goddess of Western Christendom. Yet, despite the identification of the Black Madonna with the body, with the earth, with the chthonic, there was just as much sentimentality about her restorative powers as if she were the blue-gowned Virgin herself. In fact, the dark side of the mother goddess is not just body and earth; she is disease, depression, despair, desiccation, dissolution, descent and . . . death. As a poet reminds us,

> I know the colour rose, and it is lovely,
> but not when it ripens in a tumour;
> and healing greens, leaves and grass, so springlike,
> in limbs that fester are not springlike.[49]

---

[48] *Being and Time*, p. 353.
[49] Dannie Abse, "Pathology of Colors," in J. Paul Hunter, ed., *The Norton Introduction to Poetry*, p. 156.

The unsentimental worship of the goddess requires an acknowledgment of the cycle of sacrifice which, along with the developmental imago of the quest, is one of the two great organizing mythologems of humankind.[50] The giver of life is unambiguously personified in the Hindu Kali, with her necklace of skulls. "The force that through the green fuse drives the flower . . . / is my destroyer," Dylan Thomas observed.[51] We all kill to survive, and Death, or the Black Madonna, devours us all the time. We carnivores and herbivores eat as we are being eaten. We break the gods' and goddess' bodies into our daily bread (transforming Ceres, goddess of the grains, into cereal); we crush grapes into wine (reconstituting dismembered Dionysus, who may liberate, or obscure, our flagging spirits). Those who remember such ancient dramas, the reciprocity of death and life, know that they participate in a larger order of meaning. Those who do not, go in fear of death and in fear of life. Jung amplifies this paradox:

> People who most feared life when they were young . . . suffer later just as much from the fear of death. When they are young one says they have infantile resistances against the normal demands of life; one should really say the same thing when they are old, for they are likewise afraid of one of life's normal demands. We are so convinced that death is simply the end of a process that it does not ordinarily occur to us to conceive of death as a goal and a fulfillment, as we do without hesitation the aims and purposes of youthful life in its ascendance.[52]

One of those goals would seem to be the fulfillment of the teleology of the Great Mother, however reluctant the ego.

What we call the Black Madonna is a grudging acknowledg-

---

[50] See Hollis, *Tracking the Gods,* for a discussion of how these two mythologems organize human behavior and create the spiritual dynamics of culture and of individual life.

[51] *Collected Poems,* p. 10.

[52] "The Soul and Death," *The Structure and Dynamics of the Psyche,* CW 8, par. 797.

ment of the dark side of nature, itself a grudging acknowledgment of the dark side of God, which in turn is a grudging acknowledgment of the mysterious identity of life and death.

Only the timorous ego makes this split; the gods do not. To
align ourselves against this cycle is surely the most self-
defeating, neurotic move possible, and yet how familiar it is to us
all. It is quite natural for the ego, fragile construct that it is, both
bully and coward, alternately brave and foolish, servant of sundry
complexes, to deny whatever overwhelms it. How could the ego
get out of bed every morning, metaphorically speaking, knowing
it was doomed, without some capacity for denial?

Yet in that denial, that splitting from natural reality, we also
hinder our move toward consciousness, our urgency for meaning,
our obligation to make value choices. Did not the English essay-
ist Samuel Johnson observe that there is nothing like the threat
of the noose to quicken the mind? And in that quickening, are
we not most human, most differentiated from the lowly slug?

So denial is understandable, but also immensely damaging to
the life we live. Certainly death as quickener is the frequent
catalyst for urgency of choice. Are we not like the lowly fireflies
whose brief flame is the source of the next generation?

> The firefly light pattern is a mating signal. Males blink a certain se-
> quence and hope to see an answering flash from a female. Each of the
> 200 species have their own signal. . . . Fireflies live for two years as
> larvae, eating worms from the soil, and for just two weeks as
> adults—enjoying just 14 nights of flying, flashing and courtship,
> then it is all over. "For them, it is a very short, intense time."[53]

As for them, so for us: a short, intense time.

Where are we, then, with this death business? Should we not
run as hard and as long as we can? Should we not go shopping?
Eat more? Or, let's say we are not denying death, but that, like
Woody Allen, we prefer not to be there when it happens.

---

[53] Paul Recer, "Scientists Solve Firefly Mystery."

If we find ourselves in our own Gardens of Gethsemane, do we not wish to have this individuation business without Golgotha too? But do they not necessarily go together? Allegedly, the last remark of Henry James, as his death approached, was, "Ah . . . the Distinguished Thing . . . ." It certainly sounds like James. If he did not say it, I think he would have wanted to.

Perhaps the model of Socrates is most instructive. In the three dialogues titled *Apology*, *Crito* and *Phaedo*, we learn from Plato that the Sage of Athens was condemned by the citizens for alleged impieties and for corrupting the youth. In his defense Socrates proclaimed his great reverence for the gods, his life-long devotion to learning their will, and his cultivation of a humbling curiosity in the young. Alas, his questioning of established values had gored more than one politician's ox. In the end he was condemned to die by a vote of 280 to 220. While his disciples argued that he should flee such an obviously biased judgment, Socrates responded that he had committed himself to abide by the laws of his city-state and so he would accept the decision of its authorities. Similarly, he argued against revenge and flight as being ignoble.

Paradoxically, Socrates argued that the philosopher always pursues death, for it is the great mystery. He intuited ideas of time and space of which he had no direct experience, and he believed that the psyche (soul) survives its material existence. He saw death, then, as freedom from the limits of the senses, a liberation rather than a defeat. He believed that if there was an afterlife, he would pursue his questions with renewed vigor, and enjoy meeting Homer, Hesiod and other great souls who had preceded him. If there was only perpetual sleep, he could use the rest. As for injustice, he noted that no one can make the just person unjust, and Athens would have to answer for its suppression of one of its most loyal citizens, one who cared enough to examine the fundamental premises upon which its civilization was founded.

What we see in Socrates, then, is the portrait of a person who

98 So . . . Ahem, What's This Death Business?

above all maintained the dignity of his journey. Victim of injustice, as sooner or later we all are, he held to his values. He created a life which made sense to him, even if it confused and threatened others. He lived with passion, with dignity, with courage, with integrity. And in the end, he faced death as he had lived life, for to him they constituted a seamless web.

Socrates decided what was important to him and lived it out. No institution or family of origin can determine what matters most for another. He lived his life and his death in concert with his values. He was the sum of his choices. And his choices still provide a paradigm of personhood still. In the face of death, the too-small shoes Jung described are all too attractive. But Socrates, in his life and in his death, consciously stepped into the largeness of the journey.

Whatever we may think of Socrates, we need to recall one obvious fact: *Whatever death is, anything we think or feel about it now is literally irrelevant.* Either the ego is transformed into eternity (as Socrates implied), which lies beyond our capacities to comprehend, or it is annihilated, whereby the existential angst is obviated, as is every concern that currently distresses us. If there is an afterlife, then it is a life other than this one, and will be lived according to its different conditions. If death is annihilation, then we are returned to the status of the fireflies with but few nights, and a fleeting flame.

Though he does not figure large in the literature of thanatology, one of the most profound of witnesses to this question is Jung. He believed that life should always be lived forward, with a prospective attitude, for that best serves the principle of development. We all know people who lament the loss of the good old days, days which they no doubt lamented for their difficulty at the time. They cling to the music of the past, the mores of the past, the attitudes of the past. While this nostalgia is understandable, it is also regressive. When we remember that the word "nostalgia" comes from the Greek *nostos,* meaning "pain for home," we understand both its appeal and its danger.

Of course we may wish to value friends, places, experiences of the past. Carrying them with us is how we honor their worth to us. But nostalgia is also an excuse for avoiding growth, for refusing to pick up the next stage of our journey, especially its painful parts. To commit to love another is also to commit to their loss, for one will inevitably leave the other. To commit to growth means that one will have to leave safe places and venture into the unknown. But that is where the soul will enlarge.

When we consider that we cannot avoid the choice between anxiety and depression, the former being the price of growth, the latter the fee for regression, then we must choose the anxious path in order to grow. Some of the creative spirits we most admire—Yeats, Henry Moore, Picasso, the list is endless— continued to fling themselves against their own limitations in their advanced years.

No one has spoken more eloquently than Jung on the psychology of the second half of life. Our society prepares us for the first half by calling us to an identification with roles— partner, wage-earner, parent—but gives almost no direction for the second half.

> We have no schools for forty year olds. . . . Our religions were always such schools in the past, but how many people regard them like that today? . . . A human being would certainly not grow to be seventy or eighty years old if this longevity had no meaning for the species. . . . Whoever carries over into the afternoon the law of the morning . . . must pay for it with damage to his soul.[54]

So much for nostalgia.

No wonder so many of us feel betrayed in the second half of life as the power of our roles to embody the totality of psychic energy wanes. No wonder one grows nostalgic for a time when the rules seemed clearer, the goals attainable, and the rewards worthwhile. Yet, as Jung says, to cling to the psychology and

---

[54] "The Stages of Life," *The Structure and Dynamics of the Psyche,* CW 8, pars. 786f.

attitudes of the first half of life is to damage the soul. That is a powerful summons to personal growth.

The second half of life may certainly still include goals, but hopefully more appropriate ones. They will prize depth over abundance; wisdom over knowledge; humility over arrogance; experimentation over security; growth over comfort; meaning over peace of mind. As Jung suggests,

> From the standpoint of psychotherapy it would . . . be desirable to think of death as only a transition, as part of a life process whose extent and duration are beyond our knowledge.[55]

Some of Jung's most important reflections on death are to be found in his 1934 essay "The Soul and Death." It bears some summation here, for it speaks so eloquently of our dilemma. Jung is unsparing. "People who most feared life when they were young," he says, "suffer later just as much from the fear of death."[56] To understand his point we must look into our historic attitude toward the ambiguity of life itself.

While we would interpret the youth's aversion to life's demands as a neurosis, a dominating complex, so we also need to see the adult's aversion to the transitus of death as a shrinking from life. While we accepted the fantasy of youthful achievement, health and imperialistic expansion without question, as though rightfully ordained, we inconsistently shrink from the idea of death as a purposeful goal. Understandable as are our efforts to forestall our eventual demise, we cannot have it both ways, though our youth-obsessed culture encourages us to think so. Having it both ways is what we quaintly call neurosis. In its denial, contemporary culture is essentially neurotic.

---

[55] Ibid., par. 792. My own recognition of this "afternoon imperative" has led me to work analytically only with those in the second half of life, and to work for the C.G. Jung Educational Center of Houston, which offers many courses and conferences each year to foster personal growth and public education.
[56] "The Soul and Deat," *The Structure and Dynamics of the Psyche,* CW 8, par. 797.

One thread of that neurosis may be found in our revealing metaphors of death as enemy rather than natural companion, or as completion. Poised in an heroic posture against the robed guy with the scythe, we are trapped in a fantasy which can only end in defeat. We are all grateful for penicillin, CAT-scans, heart bypasses, kidney transplants and the like, but the end will come, whether now or later. As T.S. Eliot writes (alluding to Andrew Marvel before him), "But at my back in a cold blast I hear / The rattle of the bones, and chuckle spread from ear to ear."[57]

Whatever contradicts nature, then, does a grave disservice to the soul. Again, Jung:

> Natural life is the nourishing soil of the soul. Anyone who fails to
> go along with life remains suspended, stiff and rigid in midair. That
> is why so many people get wooden in old age; they look back and
> cling to the past with a secret fear of death in their hearts . . . . but
> no living relation to the present. From the middle of life onward,
> only he remains vitally alive who is ready to *die with life.*[58]

If our personal psychology is fear based, as it often is, and denies our ultimate reality, how healthy can that be? What fine fruit falls from a poisoned tree? The building of empire, the expectations placed on partners and children for gratification, the flights into fantasies of immortality—all take us further from ourselves and whatever meaning we may chance to find in the fulfillment of our journeys.

The question of what awaits us "in the end" must be left to later, when it might or might not be answered in a manner ego can experience. While there are those who by reason of faith or some personal experience are convinced of an afterlife, most of us will have to wait to find out personally what Henry James reportedly addressed as "the Distinguished Thing."

Jung himself walks a fine line on this question. He does not

---

[57] "The Wasteland," in *The Complete Poems and Plays: 1909-1952,* pp. 42f.
[58] "The Soul and Death," *The Structure and Dynamics of the Psyche,* CW 8, par. 800.

ask us to accept something so important on his recommendation alone. "I shall certainly not assert now that one must believe death to be a second birth leading to survival beyond the grave."[59] However, he notes that human history, including all the world religions, offers intimations of immortality. It is the easy temptation of the modern rational tradition, following Freud, to deny the possibility of transformed survival. Freud said of that "oceanic feeling," which he associated with religious experience, that he simply had never felt it. And Jung replies:

> At some time someone is supposed to have invented a God and sundry dogmas and to have led humanity around by the nose with this "wish-fulfilling" fantasy. But this opinion is contradicted by the psychological fact that the head is a particularly inadequate organ when it comes to thinking up religious symbols. They do not come from the head at all, but from some other place, perhaps the heart; certainly from a deep psychic level very little resembling consciousness. . . . That is why religious symbols have a distinctly "revelatory" character. . . . They are anything rather than thought up; on the contrary, . . . they have developed, plant-like, as natural manifestations of the human psyche.[60]

Jung is not making a metaphysical assertion here; he is recognizing that what is indisputable for us psychologically is the autonomous symbol-making function that brings us closer to the mystery. The *idea* of an afterlife is psychologically compelling because it is ubiquitous. It is not that a consensus has the final word, lest the moon be ruled cheese, Elvis still alive, and aliens lurk among us, but that what activates a person's psyche is real for that person and constitutes his or her meaning. Remember the woman who said she lived on the moon? She did.

Jung adds:

> Experience shows that religions are in no sense conscious constructions, but that they arise from the natural life of the unconscious

---

59 Ibid., par. 804.
60 Ibid., par. 805.

psyche and somehow give adequate expression to it. This explains their universal distribution and their enormous influence on humanity throughout history, which would be incomprehensible if religious symbols were not at the very least truths of man's psychological nature.[61]

Symbols arise from deep within us. They tell us of the guiding energies of the cosmos, of which our psyche is a small personal part. For those who want certainty, let them find a group of like-minded folks, take a vote, and decide once and for all. Their vote will have no bearing on reality, of course, and their strident dogmatism will only reveal the anxiety that underlies their unconscious fears of the unknown. The rest of us are better off abiding the mystery and being enlarged by the question.

Every morning and every evening I "talk" to my beloved dog Shadrach, who died in my arms some years ago. I speak to my parents too, also long gone. I do not know if he or they exist in some other realm, but I do know that they are not dead to me. I acknowledge and honor their continued presence in my life. This is not sentimentality; it is testimony to the fact that though death ends one kind of relationship, it does not touch another.

Jung has been criticized for "psychologizing" religion, meaning that religious beliefs are *only* psychological. This is unfair. For Jung, the psyche is the only reality we can know, and he honors all its manifestations. He believes that

nervous disorders consist primarily in an alienation from one's instincts, a splitting off of consciousness from certain basic facts of the psyche. Hence rationalistic opinions come unexpectedly close to neurotic symptoms.[62]

Furthermore, since our nature from the moment of our creation is already hurtling us toward mortality, he says:

It is a matter of indifference what the individual consciousness may

---

[61] Ibid.

[62] Ibid., par. 808.

think about it. But subjectively it makes an enormous difference whether consciousness keeps in step with the psyche or whether it clings to opinions of which the heart knows nothing.[63]

It was Jung's clinical experience (and is mine as well) that the overtly dying do not dream of endings. They dream of journeys, crossings, recovery. All of us dream of dying, but this seldom points to one's bodily death; rather it is the psyche's way of giving notice that some attitude or stage of life is to be supplanted by another. So Jung says,

> I was astonished to see how little ado the unconscious psyche makes of death. It would seem as though death were something relatively unimportant, or perhaps our psyche does not bother about what happens to the individual. But it seems that the unconscious is all the more interested in *how* one dies; that is, whether the attitude of consciousness is adjusted to dying or not.[64]

Just as the psyche disregards the limits of time and space, so we are asked to reframe our ego's nervous feelings about "the end." How we approach the meaning of our journey is closely tied to how mindful we are of our mortality. Such mindfulness is not morbid; it quickens consciousness, helps us differentiate the trivial from the enduring, calls us to choice rather than vacillation, and, in the face of annihilation, relocates us in the context of compelling mystery.

We all find daily ways to deny, postpone, transcend this death business. It is quite natural for consciousness, so painfully won, to deny its own extinction. Catharine Pickstock writes of the French philosopher Jacques Derrida:

> In an essay entitled *Aporias*, a deconstruction of Heidegger's analysis of death in *Being and Time*, Derrida, following Blanchot, argues that death cannot be approached phenomenologically because it does not "appear," and so one cannot have a "more" or "less" authentic

---

[63] Ibid.
[64] Ibid., par. 809.

relationship with something that does not appear, which is to say, with the radically unknown and unknowable.[65]

She goes on to say that "in effect he makes the fact that death is unknown equal to the fact that death is nothing."[66]

Nothing may be no-thing, but it is not nothing. Obviously death is wholly other, radically unknown, and from the ego position unknowable, a journey from which no traveler has returned.

But is death truly "other"? Think about it. Is death not our daily companion? We have all died many deaths. Not only does each day die with sleep, and each sexual congress with "the little death," as the saying goes, but even these current, contemplative, cognitive cells are dying. Memory too is dying, who we were is dying; and yet life is somehow, inexplicably, served by each dying. Each of us is here, in this moment, yet each prone to the turn of Fortune's Wheel. Indeed, it is the nature of life to include, even demand, this ongoing death.

There are many ways of dying. Death is only one of them. Jung concludes that "deviation from the truths of the blood begets neurotic restlessness. . . . Restlessness begets meaninglessness, and the lack of meaning in life is a soul-sickness."[67] How one lives, inextricably tied to how one experiences the immanence of non-being in the midst of being, is what gives depth and dignity to the journey.

The Greek myth of Tithonus tells us that the godly gift of immortality made his choices hollow and his life restless, merely repetitive and profoundly meaningless. Upon his petition, he was granted mortality so that his life and his choices might have meaning again. We, too, have been so blessed by the gods. Is that something we can tolerate, to have been blessed by the gods? Dare we have religious experience after all? And can we tolerate

---

[65] *After Writing: On the Liturgical Consummation of Philosophy*, p. 108.

[66] Ibid., p. 109.

[67] "The Soul and Death," *The Structure and Dynamics of the Psyche*, CW 8, par. 815.

such a deep, dark gift? As Rilke concludes in one of his sonnets to Orpheus:

> Only those who have lifted their Lyre
> amid these shadows
> may intimate
> eternal Praise.[68]

So, now, how da ya like yer blue-eyed boy, O Distinguished Thing?
Ah . . . Ahem . . . .

---

[68] "Sonnets to Orpheus," I, 9. (Author's translation).

9
What Supports Me?

Believing is not quite
needing to believe, I suppose.
There you are, though,
one of the faithful
waiting—wearing a tie
and your only good suit.
— Nickole Ingram, "Soul-Mate."

To the question: what supports you, one person will say "God," another, "Nothing," and a college student, "My parents."

Push either of the first two parties and they will get very vague, very quickly, and formulaic. The idea of God is for most simply a concept, a convenient and conventional way of avoiding the question, not a felt experience. The notion of "nothing" is equally vague and avoids the obvious fact that something does bring us into this journey, autonomously directs a developmental process at both the cellular and spiritual levels, occasions consciousness as an epiphenomenon, and obliges us to ask such questions as, "What supports me?" The pearl is generated from the irritant in the mucous membrane of the mollusk. Our works of beauty, our spirituality, even our bestialities, are similarly occasioned by the irritant of this question in our psychic membranes.

I recently had the privilege of participating in a conference in Assisi, Italy, on the subject of the confluence of matter and spirit, having to do with the meeting place of depth psychology and the so-called new sciences, including quantum physics, chaos theory and systems analysis. One discussion revolved around the technology of holography, whereby a laser beam is fractionated and strikes an object at multiple levels simultaneously, creating the illusion of depth and a third dimension, even though it is represented on a two-dimensional surface.[69]

It occurred to me that holography raises anew an ancient debate about the nature of reality, the interactive space between subject and object, between viewer and viewed. Plato argued that the particular object was available to consciousness only because it participated in the larger Idea, its archetypal fundament, while Aristotle argued the reverse, that the particular object was itself the reality from which our cumulative experience made categories possible.

Holography seems to return the depth dimension to our experience, but does it? Since we were in Assisi, with the great works of Giotto at the top of the hill in the looming Basilica, it seemed germane to me to review our relationship to the object. Art historians consider Giotto the hinge upon which swings a shift in Western sensibility, the turn from art as iconography to art as embodiment. So-called medieval art served a mostly illiterate public, depicting Biblical stories as icons, objects which summon the observer to a thought, to a belief, especially to a belief about the relative unimportance of this brief transit and the far greater importance of the world beyond.

With Giotto one sees the development of perspective, the *trompe l'oeil* which implies depth on a two-dimensional surface. One sees the shadowing of faces to suggest their volume. One sees the progressive embodiment of the objective world and with it a commitment to a this-worldly *Weltanschauung*, and a respect for the objective which, among other things, furthered the development of the natural and social sciences. One can see this whole drama in Giotto's great frescos on the walls of the Basilica atop the hill.

For centuries after Giotto, it was the presumed task of the

---

[69] The shifting images on some credit cards are common examples. (The word "laser" is an acronym for Light Amplification by Stimulated Emission of Radiation.) For a practical description of how to make a simple hologram, see Daryl Sharp, *Chicken Little: The Inside Story,* pp. 109ff.

artist to embody this world, to treat the object in such fashion as to allow us to participate in the illusion that we are seeing something objective. In addition to the representations of dogma, one sees the unfolding of a progressively widening range of interest in the objects of the world. The Virgins in Caravaggio's work, for example, are fleshly, drawn from his prostitute model, and interesting in and for themselves far more than for whatever dogma they illustrate. In short, we are interested in *her,* not in her allegorical role as the Virgin.

Over the next centuries, the subject of art seems to be the "real" world: political events, such as David's portrait of the crowning of Napoleon, or Uccello's depiction of a Florentine battle, or Corot and the Barbizon school's celebration of woods and streams, or scenes of peasant life as in Breughel, or portraits of individual worthies, whether seen through the eyes of Bronzini, Durer or Holbein.

All along the artist has known better. All art is a *trompe l'oeil,* an arrangement of color and form on a surface, a two-dimensional assemblage that activates our psyches and creates an interactive space between observer and observed. Art invites us to enter a deliberate *folie à deux* of aesthetic communion. With the invention of the daguerreotype in the 1830s, however, the game is up. The artist is freed from enslavement to the object by the development of photography. Now he or she could leave the piles of dead at Antietam Creek to Matthew Brady's crews, and the portraits of the famous to the darkrooms which sprang up in every city.

Those we call Impressionists today were the first to take full advantage of this freedom from enslavement to the object.[70] What the impressionists knew was that we do not even see the

---

[70] Ironically, Impressionism was once a term of derision because their critics, still mired in the old delusion that the task of art is faithfully to render the object, considered the work of Monet, Manet and others as mere "impressions," not finished works.

object; rather we see the light refracted and reflected back to our optic nerves by variegated molecular structures. Long before lasers, they intuited the amplification and refraction of light which radiated from objects. Their subject, then, was not the object, but light itself, as one sees in the anticipatory work of England's J.M.W. Turner. Their great gift is an old, old trick: to convey for the moment that reality is a mass of stable light, even while light itself is energy and not mass.

This freedom from enslavement to the literalization of the object was quickly followed by the Pointillists who broke light down into its component parts, favoring particle theory over wave theory. The disassembling of the object was furthered by Cezanne, who broke apart the object into its planes and made Cubism possible. The Cubists testify that what we see are surfaces, angles of relationship, whether in a hillside or a human face. The Expressionists and the Vorticists remind us that what we are seeing is not static material, but energy.

The Dadaists wished to celebrate the final liberation from the object and from allusive subject matter by embracing absurdity, found objects and unnatural gatherings of perception. The Surrealists like Magritte, Tanguy and Dali quickly picked up the message (espoused by both Freud and Jung) that reality is what the psyche embodies, not what the mind expects. The bizarre imagery of dreams is, in the end, more real in its nonlogical assemblage than one's perceptions of the external world. Dreams serve the logic of the psyche rather than the logic of consciousness. By our era, art has been fully liberated from enslavement to the object by abstraction and abstract expressionism. The foremost proponent of the latter, Jackson Pollock, was in Jungian analysis. His demons were no less real than Massacio's in Florence's Santa Maria del Carmine, but his canvases do not purport to return us to the delusory object.

Holography, which brings a new sophistication of technology to the object, tricks us again into the illusion of depth. Though it promises the gift of the third dimension, in fact, on its two-dimensional surface the holographic objective world disappears as quickly as we change our angle of view. So we are back in psyche's realm once again. The ego has been seduced into its old fantasy of world domination, and quickly becomes a prisoner of its own delusion. As many modern artists have shown us, the center has been entirely relocated from the object to the psyche. Our task, then, is for psyche to be able to reflect on itself even while remaining the subject of its own reflection. As vertiginous as this relocation may be, we have been restored to mystery, to the interactive space where our limited consciousness is confronted by, guess what, *whatever supports us.*

Modern art, in its dethronement of the object, recalls us to the notion of Teilhard de Chardin that matter is spirit moving slowly enough to be seen. Naturally, the old ego wishes to freeze and fix that movement, to own it. As in our theologies, the moment we think we have the gods pinned down, they have already gone underground. The more we presume the ego's sovereignty, the more we breed monsters. Sadly, more people have been killed in the name of religion than for all other causes put together.

Few of us will likely go off to die for, or slay others for, the superiority of our metaphor, but when we forget that what supports us is invisible, we fall into the heresy of literalism. Where symbol and metaphor point toward mystery, banners and dogma point toward delusory literalism. And many have and will suffer because of someone else's inability to tolerate the invisible world which supports the visible world. Where once tribal myth pointed toward, and embodied, such invisible energy, now we are forced to become psychological. Since not many of us want to take on the responsibility for being psychological after all, much of contemporary politics and institutional religion is just as polarizing, noninclusive and fragmenting as the old city-states of Umbria and the Wars of the Roses.

A more concrete manifestation of this unwillingness to abide, tolerate and dialogue with the invisible world is manifested in modern psychology and psychiatry. While there is much, much good to be derived from the modification of behaviors, from the reprogramming of antiquated cognitive messages, and from bio-chemical rebalancing, the resulting fragmentation of the person which is practiced by most modern therapies, and is most pleasing to insurance companies, is a profound failure of nerve, an act of moral cowardice in the face of the largeness of the mystery that we all embody. The belief that someone is the sum of his or her behavior, attitudes and chemistry is insulting.

And so our contemporary healing armamentarium insults us in such an unconscious fashion.

What produces change in us, growth, healing? Essentially we do not know. Freud even threw up his hands toward the end of his life and said, for all his interest in technique and interpretation, that it was love that heals. The central metaphor of the last four centuries has been that of the machine. We have gained obvious mastery of aspects of material life, from health to transportation to communication, through the machine. We even compare our brains to computers, the same brains that created the computers. But we are not machines. Our changes, our agendas, our summons to growth, are not mere mechanics. Therapy is not engineering.

Our complexes are not just bad chips that need replacements. Our instincts are not just hard wiring in the main frame which needs retooling. Our behaviors are not just bad programs, discardable three-and-a-half inch floppies. Put all those pieces together and *we* are still left over.

As everyone knows, for all our material progress, happiness is even further away; moral compasses are left in the hands of the small minded and fearful, with the great angst of spiritual dislocation the central fact of our time. Awash as we are in material abundance, we are more lost than any who have gone before.

Ironically, the archaic language of the ancient world is more useful than any modern terminology or instrumentality. If we bring our history and our consciousness together, much of great worth will be learned. Though, as we all know, healing, or the recovery of meaning, is not always assured. (T.S. Eliot's "The Love Song of J. Alfred Prufrock" provides a perfect example of a person of high moral intent and quickened consciousness who was utterly, regressively, defeated by himself). Whatever healing is, whatever meaning may occur which supports us, we cannot engineer either by ego alone. What we call meditation, therapy or sometimes even friendship, is an interactive encounter with that energy which supports us. Such occasions, to use the old language, is to invite the gods to be present. And sometimes they come. The healing of the person, and the healing of the world, the *Tikkun Olam*, will not occur without the presence of those energies we metaphorically call the gods.

Bring consciousness and history together and we have a good start. But what we seek in depth therapy, and what humans historically invited through prayer and religious ritual, is the activation of "the third." This is not governed by technique or interpretation, as useful as these may be. The third is the spontaneous emergence of a quantum of energy that manifests in such fashion as may repair the wounding. In other words, the process of healing always requires the activation of the gods who once, in popular imagination, walked in physical form, and who today we experience as energy.

I do not say that the metaphor of humans as machines is completely useless, but the limitation of that metaphor is the oldest of religious sins: the seduction of idolatry. When Dante placed the gluttonous in the Inferno, for example, he was not against food. He was mindful of metaphor. The deadly sin of gluttony resulted from the relocation of what ultimately nourishes from the invisible world to the visible, from the godly realm to its reification in the worship of food.

Similarly, in Dante's view, when the materialists achieve what they wish and are condemned to push boulders through eternity, when the wrathful are encased in the fire of their fury, when the slothful drown and so on, it is as much to say that they have forgotten the third, the gods who come to us as energy and not matter. They remain enslaved by the object, seduced by the material world, lacking relationship to the elusive transcendent.

It is in the recovery of our appreciation for the world as energy that depth psychology and the new sciences meet. It may eventually occur to us that some metaphor other than "energy" will serve us better. But for now, energy works to remind us that the objects around us, the natural world, we ourselves, are all a swirling assemblage of energy whose purposiveness greatly transcends that of which we can be conscious.

Just as vocation is found by serving one's *daimon*, so the meaning of our lives, our goal, is found in the movement of that energy. And all this time we thought we were adrift. Yes, it is true that we have lost the old mythological points of reference, the longitudes and latitudes of the soul which once helped our tribal ancestors map their journeys. But we now have a greater possibility of recovering the place from which all such images emerge—the psyche.

Jung writes:

> Life has always seemed to me like a plant that lives on its rhizome. Its true life is invisible, hidden in the rhizome. The part that appears above ground lasts only a single summer. Then it withers away—an ephemeral apparition. When we think of the unending growth and decay of life and civilizations, we cannot escape the impression of absolute nullity. Yet I have never lost a sense of something that lives and endures underneath the eternal flux. What we see is the blossom, which passes. The rhizome remains.[71]

Naturally, each of us seeks the purpose of our unique journey, and well we should. We betray the larger potential of our incarnation if we do not individuate. But Jung reminds us that, for all our individuality, we are common carriers of a universal energy: "Ultimately, every individual life is at the same time the eternal

---

[71] *Memories, Dreams, Reflections,* p. 4.

life of the species."[72]

Typically, for Jung, the opposites hold true. We are profoundly alone, individual, separate, and, as the old Chippewa song has it, carried on great winds across the sky. Our role in the big picture is a mystery. The events of our lives, so important in the moment, are so transient when seen at some remove. And yet, as Gerard Manley Hopkins noted of carbon, the fundament of matter, this diamond that we all are: "This Jack, joke, poor potsherd, patch, matchwood, immortal diamond, / Is immortal diamond."[73]

Nothing is more elemental than carbon, the pivot of organic chemistry, but how that carbon is energized, and to what end, is our mystery and our persisting conundrum. As Jung concludes of this question of what moves, carries and supports us: "In the end the only events of my life worth telling are those when the imperishable world irrupted into this transitory one."[74]

In the end, when the dust settles and the carbon disassembles, may it be known that we were here, and became, if only through the presence of these questions, something more, much more, than dust.

---

[72] "Psychology and Religion," *Psychology and Religion,* CW 11, par. 146.
[73] "That Nature is a Heraclitean Fire and the Comfort of the Resurrection," *A Hopkins Reader,* p. 81.
[74] *Memories, Dreams, Reflections,* p. 4.

10
What Matters, in the End?

"Who are you really, wanderer?"—
and the answer you have to give
no matter how dark and cold
the world is around you is:
"Maybe I'm a king."
— William Stafford, "A Story that Could be True."

The progress of life is sustained by projection, without which we would succumb to torpor and depression. Projection is invariably present in all new moments, for we seek to understand the new, to manage it, by what we have known of the old.

As noted earlier, projections and transference are the chief sources of repetition in our lives, the cause of stuckness as much as of forward motion. Yet projection is unavoidable and does move us into life. In the first half of life the power of a projection to offer security, personal identity, the satisfaction of emotional needs, does direct libido in the service of our development. By midlife, those same projections may exhaust themselves; our energy falls back into the unconscious, manifesting symptomatically as boredom or depression. Perhaps the most powerful of our projections, the one that gets us out of bed and inspirits our journey, is the idea that there is somewhere to go, something to do, some place where all will be well.

If we are to use the metaphor of life as journey at all, then whither are we going? What is the goal, the end place, the safe harbor, the *raison d'être* for this massive effort? In his classic account of his own journey, Peter Matthiessen writes of our common search and of that

> nostalgia, not for home or place, but for lost innocence—the paradise
> lost that . . . is the only paradise. Childhood is full of mystery and

116

promise, and perhaps the life fear comes when all the mysteries are laid open, when what we thought we wanted is attained. It is just at the moment of seeming fulfillment that we sense irrevocable betrayal, like a great wave rising silently behind us, and we know most poignantly . . . "all worldly pursuits have but one unavoidable and inevitable end, which is sorrow: acquisitions end in dispersion; buildings in destruction; meetings in separation; births, in death. . . ." Confronted by the uncouth spectre of old age, disease, and death, we are thrown back upon the present, on this moment, here, right now, for that is all there is.[75]

Consider this delightful description of the etymology of the word "nostalgia":

There are two constant and opposing cries. One the poet has phrased:

I want to take the next train out,
No matter where it's going.

The other is as directly put in the words of any child: "I wanna go home!" Nostalgia is a literal translation of the latter feeling. It is from Gr. *nostos,* return home, + *algos,* pain (as also in *neuralgia,* nerve pain, etc.). Odysseus was an early sufferer.[76]

Chances are that readers of this book are nostalgic for a time when their projections were vital and energizing, a time when one expected to one day arrive at some good place. Yet by this time, many such readers will have achieved the goal of those projections and found life still unsatisfying and elusive, or recognized the impossibility of their fulfillment.

There was a time when "California" was the goal, the luminous land of beginnings. Now we are there. Los Angeles is two Newarks; Oakland, according to Gertrude Stein, has no "there" there, and, amid rolling power blackouts, California may fall off into the Pacific if the pollution does not take everyone first. I mean no disrespect to California, or Californians, of course; this

---

[75] *The Snow Leopard,* pp. 132f.
[76] Joseph T. Shipley, *Dictionary of Word Origins,* p. 244.

is simply a metaphor for the achievement of one's goal, arriving only to find that one has not arrived anywhere. Is there somewhere else one needs to go, then, when one has reached whatever California once promised?

Theoretically, one could renew projections repeatedly. The *right* person is out there who will free us, succor us, parent us. The *right* job, the *right* home, the *right* ideology . . . surely just over the next horizon? Once one has become conscious of projections, has come to consciousness amid the wreckage of bad choices, begun to sense the lurking presence of Henry James's "Distinguished Thing," is there any alternative to depression, distracting entertainment and spiritual nihilism? It is tempting to give it all up. Yet, such spiritual uncertainty does not mean the question goes away. It simply goes underground and eventuates as sociopathy, depression or at best as symbolic expression. On this subject, Jung writes:

> Any uncertainty about the God-image causes a profound uneasiness in the self, for which reason the question is generally ignored because of its painfulness. But that does not mean that it remains unasked in the unconscious. What is more, it is answered by views and beliefs like materialism, atheism, and similar substitutes which spread like epidemics.[77]

Stephen Dunn writes in his Pulitzer Prize-winning volume:

> It's time to give up the search for the invisible.
> On the best of days there's little more
> than the faintest intimations . . . .
> I think I'll keep on describing things
> to ensure that they really happened.[78]

Yet, ever in pursuit of such intimations, Dunn's work is obsessed by the invisible. Even as he celebrates the sensual present, the tangible surface which brings pain or pleasure, and a evanes-

---

[77] *Aion,* CW 9ii, par. 170.
[78] "Sixty," in *Different Hours,* p. 22.

cent sense of the real, the desire for the invisible remains—unforgettable, insistent. However much he repudiates the gods, such a man has the gods with him, is god-intoxicated, albeit obscurely, all the time. He is more faithful in his honest doubt than all the pious evangelicals who could not tolerate genuine apotheosis if it manifested before them on television in a seersucker jacket and a big hair-do, selling shoddy spiritual furniture.

There is a high price to pay for being an honest man in search of an honest god. Elsewhere Dunn writes:

> More and more you learn to live
> with the unacceptable.
> You sense the ever-hidden God
> retreating even farther,
> terrified or embarrassed.
> You might as well be a clown,
> big silly clothes, no evidence of desire.[79]

But the desire remains, coursing underground, because that is who we are—angst-laden, divinity-seeking glory-clowns who have no choice but to continue the turbulent passage across what Yeats called "that dolphin-torn, that gong-tormented sea,"[80] which resonates in our unconscious as that devil-torn, that god-tormented sea.

What matters, then, and what do we carry with us on this journey? Readers will no doubt have their own list, to which I propose to add a few items of my own. They are hardly original, but for me they provide a measure of companionship and a continuing personal agenda that keeps me on my toes.

Doing Our Work

The work we are called upon to do is not the job for which we are paid. The work, the *opus,* is the search for the gods, the search for one's vocation, the tracking of the invisible. It is the

---

[79] "Before the Sky Darkens," in ibid., p. 19.
[80] "Byzantium," in *Selected Poems and Two Plays,* p. 133.

work of private growth and private encounter. In our time, the demand for relationship is urgent, compulsive and anxious, the more so as community has eroded. Yet the paradox remains, as we have seen, that the single best thing we can do to improve our relationships is to work on ourselves, to lift off the other the impossible agenda of expectations we bring to them, to remove from them the burden of our individuation.

Recently, having been invited to give a talk to a Jung society on the theme of relationships, my hosts asked that instead of my proposed title, "The Eden Project: Psychodynamics of Relationship," might they call it "How To Improve Your Love Life"? After all, they wanted a large attendance. Friends as we are, we compromised with "LoveWork." Anything containing the word "love," that magic elixir, would guarantee an audience, but of course my focus remained on the subtitle.

A poignant illustration of the need for lovework may be found in the intersection of the personal and creative life of T.S. Eliot. Scholars have demonstrated how much poems such as "The Love Song of J. Alfred Prufrock," and even "The Wasteland," were drawn directly from his personal life (that is, his neuroses), and that he frequently quoted lines from his marital exchanges.

> "What shall I do now? What shall I do?"
> "I shall rush out as I am, and walk the street
> "With my hair down, so."[81]

And,

> "My nerves are bad to-night. Yes, bad. Stay with me.
> "Speak to me. Why do you never speak. Speak.
> "What are you thinking of? What thinking? What?
> "I never know what you are thinking. Think."[82]

Eliot carried, as we all do, a great deal of freight from his

---

[81] "The Wasteland," in *The Complete Poems and Plays, 1909-1952,* lines 131-134.
[82] Ibid., lines 111-114.

family of origin. The gifted child of a narcissistic mother, he "found" a very ill, demanding woman to marry and suffered the split, with all its symptomatic manifestations, that such a choice brings. As a recent biographer puts it:

> There is no denying that many of Eliot's early poems suggest sexual problems—not lack of desire, but inhibitions, distrust of women, and a certain physical queasiness. [His wife] Vivienne, with continuous ill health, would have been surrounded by smelly medicines, and disordered hormones led to heavy, unpredictable periods which stained the sheets. . . . After a year, he said he had been through "the most awful nightmare of anxiety that the mind of man could conceive."[83]

After turbulent bouts of madness, perhaps bipolar in nature, Vivienne was hospitalized for the rest of her life. For her, and for Eliot, we may have the most profound sympathy. However, during that long period of Vivienne's hospitalization, and even after a divorce, Eliot, racked by guilt and searching for release by a forgiving God, kept the love of his life, Emily Hale, dangling on the end of an uncertain string for decades.

For years Emily longed for marriage, traveled to England and jeopardized her academic position more than once to make herself available to him. But his complexes, maternal and marital, with an admixture of sexual guilt, kept him distanced. When Vivienne finally died in hospital, Eliot, by then elderly and ill, abruptly married his far younger secretary Valerie. Emily burned their passionate correspondence (and hurrah for her).

The point here is not to judge Eliot. He lived a miserable life, poor sod. He was dogged by demonic complexes about women, about sex, about emotional expressivity (read "Prufrock" as his self-portrait to get the picture), and he desperately, obsessively, sought a spirituality to transcend this world of pain and conflict. For this suffering we may be most empathetic.

However, he brought great grief to others, most notably to

---

[83] Lyndall Gordon, *T.S. Eliot: An Imperfect Life,* p. 124.

Emily, as a result of his inability to do his own work. That he loved her deeply there is no doubt. That he brought her great hurt, as a result of his neuroses, there is also no doubt. While we may be happy that in his final years, after his wife's death, he received a modicum of relief from his guilt, we must bemoan the grief suffered by others as a result of his blocked life.

Again, the point here is not to judge, but to be mindful of how necessary the ongoing work of healing is for each of us. Wherever we are stuck in our journey we bring hurt not only to ourselves, but to others as well. Doing our work thus becomes an ethical imperative, for it constitutes the chief good we can bring to those close to us.

Doing our work requires accepting responsibility, finding the strength to pull our projections back from others, and engaging in a dialogue with the inner world whence our life choices come. That of which I am ignorant owns me, brings repetition and misery to my life and to that of others. It is the task of a lifetime to sustain the process of sorting through these matters.

On paper, this obligation to do our own work seems obvious; in practice it is very difficult. It requires that we grow up, that we accept final responsibility for our choices and their consequences, and that we can bear the loneliness of our journey. However surrounded by others we may be, it is our private journey which no one else can take for us or rescue us from. The continued acceptance of this reality is the "lovework" demanded of us. The mystery of relationship may be found, paradoxically, in the progressively deepening encounter with the unknown beloved we ourselves are, the stranger most difficult to love.

Ask the Meaning of Your Suffering

Recall the Biblical struggle of Jacob with the Angel of Darkness. (Gen. 32:26-32) Though his limb was wrenched from its socket, Jacob would not let go until the Angel blessed him. The Angel did so "because you have been strong against God," by giving Jacob a new name: Israel.

So we are asked to confront our sufferings, to wrestle with them though that brings us even more pain, in order to know what they want of us. Just as we might interrogate a frightening figure in our dreams to learn why it has so come to us, so must we ask of our lives what task of growth is demanded. As Jung says in the passage heading this book, we are asked a question by life, and our life is a question. What does it want of us? What is demanded that we may live it more fully?

The psychodynamic view of depression is illustrative of this point. While there are different kinds of depression, some biologically based, others reactive to outer loss and so on, the kind of depression I speak of here is that which comes to us all. (Churchill called his "the black dog at the door.") The essence of the psychodynamic view of nature obliges us to acknowledge once again that we are not just the sum of behaviors, cognitions and biological processes, but that psyche is dynamic in us, and we are invited to be interactive in relating to it. Jung put it like this:

> Depression should . . . be regarded as an unconscious compensation whose content must be made conscious if it is to be fully effective. This can only be done by consciously regressing along with the depressive tendency and integrating the memories so activated into the conscious mind—which is what the depression was aiming at in the first place.[84]

This is a remarkable injunction, so radical that all these years later it is still not a part of our popular consciousness or general therapeutic practice.

Jung underlines the dynamic character of the psyche which seeks autonomously to withdraw energy from its investment in old projects and projections. We may wish to abide with the old, be safe there, but the psyche demands continuous growth and will sacrifice our comfort to achieve it. Depression is a compensation in that it obliges us to pay attention to an altered reality.

---

[84] "The Sacrifice," *Symbols of Transformation,* CW 5, par. 625.

To "consciously regress" is to go along with the depression, to swim to the bottom of the well in order to find its treasure. What we find will either oblige the investment of meaning in a new direction, one perhaps quite contrary to what the ego wishes, or that we enlarge our sensibility through the encounter with an *other* outside of our ego's volition.

Thus, for example, if we are overidentified with our work, the psyche withdraws energy from it and we are forced to define ourselves in a different way. A person who becomes depressed on retirement is being asked to see his or her journey in a new way. A person who suffers an immobilizing illness is being asked to develop a richer inner life, perhaps for the first time.

For Jung, the psyche is always teleological. It is always seeking something, most of all its own wholeness, and may not give a fig for our comforts. He writes,

> There are moments in human life when a new page is turned. New interests and tendencies appear which have hitherto received no attention, or there is a sudden change of personality . . . . the new development has drawn off the energy it needs from consciousness. This lowering of energy can be seen most clearly before the onset of certain psychoses and also in the empty stillness which precedes creative work.[85]

Even in those tumultuous bewitchments we call psychoses, or falling in love, or being seized by a core complex, or being enraged, there is meaning to be found. Our ancestors were not stupid when they asked of such a seizure, "What god is at work here?" Their intuition was that some force deeper than consciousness was active, that there was an invisible hand at work, and that one needs to come to some sort of rapprochement with it. So, too, we will often look upon so many of our difficult transitions as times when we grew the most.

Recall the betrayal of Job discussed in a previous chapter. The

---

[85] "The Psychology of the Transference," *The Practice of Psychotherapy,* CW 16, par. 373.

experience of betrayal is perpetrated as much by our own naiveté, our insufficient apprehension of complexity, as it is by the
other party. Though it is painful, that complexity serves to enlarge the personality.

Asking the meaning of our suffering tends to relocate our
sense of selfhood beyond the narrow purview of ego alone. Yes,
it is a necessary tool of consciousness, but ego alone is insufficient. By submitting to something larger than itself, ego re-
frames experience to include far more than it can ever achieve
on its own. That is why we pay attention to dreams. When psyche speaks it asks for enlargement, no matter how ambivalent
we may be about that requirement. Wrestling with the angels of
our darkness is what brings the blessing in the end. We are meant
to wrestle, not understand, not manage.

Speaking for myself, all that I believed possible in the first
half of life—complete understanding and management of life—
proved to be delusory. At midlife I was blessed by the psyche
with a deep depression. Though I did not express thanks then, I
do now. Like Eliot, I was being asked to confront old ways, life-
diminishing complexes, to open to a larger feeling life, and to
find a deeper relationship with the inner world. It was then, in
losing the fantasized sovereignty of the ego, that I encountered
the richness of the psyche.

My midlife *metanoia* appears now to have been tantamount
to a religious experience. I was obliged to stand before the depression and, humbled, ask, "What do you want of me?" That
question will always bring us a psychologically larger life. If we
hang on long enough, though it wrench our thigh from its
socket, the Dark Angel will bless us with growth, meaning and a
more interesting journey. As Jung asserts,

Analytical psychology is a reaction against the exaggerated rationali-
zation of consciousness which, seeking to control nature, isolates itself from her and so robs man of his own natural history. . . . Analytical psychology tries to resolve the resultant conflict not by going

"back to Nature" with Rousseau, but by holding on to the level of
reason we have successfully reached, and by enriching consciousness
with a knowledge of man's psychic foundations.[86]

Our ego is a necessary part of this dialogue, but consciousness
cannot be more than what history has already provided. For
growth to occur, we are required to experience the power of the
other. Going back to nature does not mean living in the wild. It
means being able to dialogue with nature and honoring it. Not to
do so breeds monsters, occasions pathology in ourselves and toward others, and narrows the range of our journey. Out of this
dialectic the path grows wider. If we can endure encounters with
those dark angels who present themselves along the way, finally
we will be blessed.

Keep Asking What Matters, in the End

Inevitably, the far greater power of the external world leads the
child to curb its potential in order to be whatever its environment demands, both to survive and, hopefully, to have one's
needs met. Essentially we have three choices: 1) to gain power
over our environment, which we do through controlling behaviors or through learning; 2) to stay out of harm's way, which we
do through avoidance or neglect of the summons to journey; or
3) to adapt, and hope for support and nurture.

There are infinite varieties of these strategies, much influenced by parental example, popular culture and individual character. Each of us has lived with such strategies for such a long
time that we up colluding in our own self-estrangement and loss
of integrity. We are all neurotic—split between the imperatives
of our nature and our adaptive habits. The reward for responding
to what the dark angels ask is to be returned to a place where the
imperative of personal journey may be recovered.

In other words, which hurt is greater—the angst-laden path of

---

[86] "Analytical Psychology and *Weltanschauung*," *The Structure and Dynamics of the Psyche,* CW 8, par. 739.

individuation in the face of the powerful environment, or the endless pain of the soul denied? What does matter, in the end?

Perhaps Jung's most succinct definition of neurosis is that it is *one-sidedness:*

> Neurosis is as a rule a pathological, one-sided development of the personality, the imperceptible beginnings of which can be traced back almost indefinitely into the earliest years of childhood.[87]

We all become one-sided in the process of adapting to whatever reality fate presents. In fact, we are often well rewarded by our culture for our one-sidedness. But with every choice of A, B and C are pushed underground and will demand to be fed one way or the other.

This is a familiar dilemma, often encouraged by the modern need for, or love of, specialization. I know of a radiologist who entered that specialty because a fellowship was available after medical school, not because he felt a calling in that direction. At midlife, he is bored, depressed, feels no engagement with patients, spends his day relating to celluloid and, in his words, "only occasionally seeing something interesting." The obvious corrective would be to change his line of work, but he is now financially secure and afraid of change. I'm afraid his depression can only get worse. Jung speaks to such a situation:

> If science is an end in itself, man's *raison d'être* lies in being a mere intellect. If art is an end in itself, then his sole value lies in the imaginative faculty, and the intellect is consigned to the lumber-room. If making money is an end in itself, both science and art can quietly shut up shop. No one can deny that our modern consciousness, in pursuing these mutually exclusive ends, has become hopelessly fragmented. The consequence is that people are trained to develop one quality only; they become tools themselves.[88]

---

[87] "The Therapeutic Value of Abreaction," *The Practice of Psychotherapy,* CW 16, par. 257.
[88] Ibid., par. 731.

If we are treat ourselves as tools instead of souls, should we be surprised when the revolt of psyche manifests in disturbing dreams, addictions, somatic invasions and depression?

Many years ago, as an academic, I often urged young people to follow their interests rather than what their parents wanted for them, or what paid best, or where jobs were plentiful. In most cases they were pressured into choices they would regret, and no doubt some of them are still prisoners of those choices many years later. Too few were encouraged or able to affirm their unique nature, to say Yes! to their soul's desired direction.

No wonder so many end up, in midlife or later, feeling betrayed. They invested in what they were led to invest in by societal pressures or, mayhap, their own constricted vision. Sometimes we hear of people making radical changes at life's critical junctures, but far more often they remain trapped by their original choices, constricted by their perceived inability to change course and embrace their soul's intent.

As a therapist I see rather more of such people than others might, but only when the pain of that inner division has become too great to deny. Even then, the focus of their therapeutic agenda is usually symptom relief. To wrestle with the dark angels, to ask what really matters, is initially beyond their imaginal horizon. My task, then, to a large extent involves reparenting and reeducation.

The reminder of the "Distinguished Thing," the limits of our lives, serves as a powerful goad. But that one is thereby all the more obliged to choose the life that is seeking to choose us still seems beyond us. We rationalize being tools, our pathologies are driven deeper, and our children are further burdened by our unlived life—the choices we were afraid to make.

To ask, every day, "What matters, in the end?" is to create the possibility of differentiated choice, the potential to overthrow the tyranny of our history, so as to honor something in us that has always been there, waiting for our courage. If we limit our aspirations to good health and making money, then we might as well, in Jung's words, "quietly shut up shop." We may feel betrayed in doing so, but we will know who the betrayer is.

If we make an effort to become conscious of our fragmented nature, we need not blindly act it out. We may thereby also be empowered to decide as grown-ups what, in the end, really matters to our soul.

Suffer Consciously

As Gautama Buddha said twenty-six centuries ago, life is suffering—but to what end, in service to what or who? This day I visited a colleague with metastasized cancer. Last week I attended the funeral of an old friend. Worrying about budget, sales figures, traffic and whether the heat will let up seems trivial. And surely it is, but compared to what? Suffering is relative, contextual and very, very personal. The great suffering of the dispossessed is so immense that most of us who live privileged lives have to turn away in order to be able to conduct our banal, quotidian lives.

Much of what passes for modern culture, as the philosopher Pascal noted even in the seventeenth century, is a vast *divertissement* from suffering. Paradoxically, it results in even more suffering as it estranges us from the deeper encounter with our journey. Some years ago I was quizzed by a woman who argued that surely the purpose of psychology is to eliminate suffering. In earlier years I might have agreed with her. But, based on subsequent personal experience, I demurred and said that often the purpose of therapy was rather to introduce one to a deeper suffering. She shook her head, perhaps writing me off as an incorrigible pessimist.

Jung also said, or at least implied, that neurosis is a flight from authentic suffering.[89] Personally, I think we suffer authentically when we experience a conflict of opposites, a conflict between duty, say, and what we really want. For example, "Should I stay in this relationship or leave it?" If one stays, one suffers the de-

---

[89] See above, p. 37.

nial of the Self; and the subsequent depression, addiction and resentment can only deepen. On the other hand, if one leaves, one will be alone, perhaps ridiculed, marginalized, consumed with doubt. So, what is the right course of action?

Suffering the tension between conflicting desires or needs or duties can lead to an awareness of what is really at stake in the context of one's larger journey. Thus, for example, one may find that the real issue is about growing up, being willing to honor what one truly wants, willing to risk criticism and rejection. As long as the underlying issues remain unconscious, one is sorely tempted to decide one way or the other, just to relieve the tension. In so doing, we perpetuate the split, suffer inauthentically, and thus are burdened with even more unlived life. Better, I think, to hold the tension until a decision manifests that is true to oneself, crystal clear. Opting out of one form of suffering, we are liable to fall into another, deeper, more pervasive suffering.

Dietrich Bonhoeffer is to my mind one of the truly admirable persons of the last century. Safely ensconced in Manhattan in a teaching position, he chose to return to his native Germany in the late 1930s and oppose the Hitler regime. He perished at Flossenburg concentration camp, murdered just before the end of the war. When so much of modern religion, with its comfortable pieties, allows one to avoid religious experience, his book *The Cost of Discipleship* continues to challenge us. Like Job, Bonhoeffer had a true encounter with divinity. Afraid for his life, as who isn't, wrestling with what his beliefs really required, as we all might, he held to the summons to a larger life, one based on values. Though he dies, yet shall he live.

The current crisis of values—the erosion of tribal myth and the inadequacy of cultural surrogates—has only deepened the meaning of suffering. Historically, such crises have always evoked regressive moves such as one sees in the religious right— the tendency toward black and white thinking, simplistic moral judgments, projection of the shadow onto the less powerful, and the acceptance of assurances that all is well even though one's neighbor is perishing. Running from honest suffering, they can't escape the pain of living a superficial life, thereby damaging both themselves and their neighbors. Jung observed,

> Once metaphysical ideas have lost their capacity to recall and evoke the original experience they have not only become useless but prove to be actual impediments on the road to wider development. One clings to possessions that have once meant wealth; and the more in-effective, incomprehensible, and lifeless they become the more obsti-nately people cling to them. . . .
>
> This end-result is . . . a false spirit of arrogance, hysteria, woolly-mindedness, criminal amorality, and doctrinaire fanaticism, a purveyor of shoddy spiritual goods, spurious art, philosophical stut-terings, and Utopian humbug, fit only to be fed wholesale to the mass man of today.[90]

Though written decades ago, does this not describe much of our contemporary scene? What used to provide spiritual wealth is now hoarded for the sake of hoarding alone. The greater the erosion, the greater the obstinacy, the compensatory arrogance, the hysteria, and the psychological coercion of others. Our spiri-tual goods are shoddy. That occasions a great, great suffering.

What is the alternative to banality, hysteria and consumer-ism? Is it not the honest, private suffering of the questions pre-sented here? Who suffers his or her own personal journey will more honestly serve the world than do those who hew to a mass ideology, be it materialism, fundamentalism or nihilism. Any ideology denies the validity of the individual soul's journey.

Let me be clear here that I am not promoting individual inter-ests over those of the collective. That would be individualism, not to be confused with individuality or individuation. Jung de-scribes the difference:

> Individualism means deliberately stressing and giving prominence to some supposed peculiarity rather than to collective considerations

---

[90] *Aion,* CW 9ii, pars. 65, 67.

and obligations. But individuation means precisely the better and more complete fulfilment of the collective qualities of the human being, since adequate consideration of the peculiarity of the individual is more conducive to a better social performance than when the peculiarity is neglected or suppressed.[91]

Again, we are led back to the paradox that feeling good may be a very poor measure of the worth of one's life. Think of those who truly contributed to the journey, those who inspired and enlarged. Feeling good was seldom part of their lives. Living the questions in a meaningful way invariably leads one to interesting places. As Jung wrote to a friend,

> The apparently unendurable conflict is proof of the rightness of your life. A life without inner contradiction is only half a life, or else a life in the Beyond, which is destined only for angels. But God loves human beings more than the angels.[92]

So that is our life, with all its contradictions and conflicts we somehow manage to endure. Suffering consciously is the only alternative to suffering unconsciously. It is a gift to oneself and, by lifting our burden off others, a gift to them as well. What we avoid in ourselves we load onto our neighbor. What we carry consciously for ourselves, frees the other. No greater love, then, than sparing our neighbor, partner, child, by consciously accepting our own suffering.

---

[91] *Two Essays on Analytical Psychology,* CW 7, par. 267.
[92] *Letters,* vol. 1, p. 375.

Conclusion
Re-Membering Psyche

What is the "psyche" of which we speak, this psyche which is exiled, ironically, from modern psychiatry, psychology, psychopathology and psychotherapy? Who re-members psyche?

Other than saying that psyche is the totality of who we are—blood, brain, viscera, history, spirit and soul—we cannot limit its meaning. Note that psyche comes from two etymological roots: that of breathing, suggestive of the invisible life force which enters at birth and departs at death; and that of the butterfly, suggesting a teleologically driven process of evolution and transformation, which in the end is both beautiful and elusive.

Certainly, in our sundered state, we intuit that re-membering psyche has something to do with our personal healing and with the healing of the world, the *Tikkun Olam*. These two are always intertwined. While we may be tempted to romanticize psyche as the place of sweet dreams, it is also the source of devouring energies, self-destruction and demonic drives. Jung observes:

> The psyche is far from being a homogenous unit—on the contrary, it is a boiling cauldron of contradictory impulses, inhibitions, and affects, and for many people the conflict between them is so insupportable that they even wish for the deliverance preached by theologians.[93]

That last clause is instructive. So intolerable is the conflict between these internal contradictions that many are seduced by totalitarian thinking of one sort or another. The flight to angels helps one avoid the commitment to this world, the work of this time and place.

---

[93] "Psychological Aspects of the Mother Archetype," *The Archetypes and the Collective Unconscious,* CW 9i, par. 190.

So, what does it mean to re-member psyche? To me it means three things: 1) that we recall we are psyche's being; 2) that we seek a dialogue with psyche which promotes healing in ourselves and others; and 3) that something wishes to re-member us.

First we recall that we are the manifestations of psyche, a unique seed of the manifold possibilities of *being* in the process of *becoming*. As Jung points out,

> The psyche is the starting-point of all human experience, and all the knowledge we have gained eventually leads back to it. The psyche is the beginning and end of all cognition. It is not only the object of its science, but the subject also. This gives psychology a unique place among all the other sciences: on the one hand there is a constant doubt as to the possibility of its being a science at all, while on the other hand psychology acquires the right to state a theoretical problem the solution of which will be one of the most difficult tasks for a future philosophy.[94]

Psyche is not homogenous, as the ego would wish and as many psychologies claim. Psyche is a congeries of experiences, an assemblage of fragments. So what keeps continuity, what keeps faith, provides consistency, provokes conscious action? As a child I wondered where we go when we sleep. Some of our ancestors believed we literally wandered outside of ourselves, but today I know that the "I" which I can know is only a small part of the greater "I" which I do not know, a "not-I" which contains even this puzzled consciousness I am wont to confuse as I.

Even memory is an uncertain guide to psyche. Not only do we forget, but we know that there are false memories and experiences which are repressed, distorted, condensed and subservient to complexes. We know that there are autonomously charged clusters of energy called complexes, some of which save our lives and some of which tie us to Ixion's wheel. But we can never escape being psychological. Everything we say, do or believe

---

[94] "Psychological Factors in Human Behavior," *The Structure and Dynamics of the Psyche,* CW 8, par. 261.

comes from this primal factory. Just as every school of psychology is a form of subjective confession of its founder, so all we produce as individuals or as a culture derives from our psychic matrix, over which ego has less and less control the more it believes in its sovereignty.

Secondly, re-membering psyche means paying attention to what it has to say—the thousand correctives which are daily found in the body, in dream images and in the historic patterns we create through our choices. Re-membering means coming home again. An analysand recently said, "Each time, I thought the next thing would bring me happiness." I asked her why she thought happiness was what psyche wanted for her. She blushed and acknowledged her indulgence in wishful thinking. But who among us has not done the same?

Most of the time, in spite of ego, psyche wants fulfillment of its own intent, larger being, incarnation in the world. These intents frequently run counter to our ego's desire for money, security, happiness or anything else. To run from that larger imperative is understandable, but it means we will never feel quite right within the sack of skin we wear.

Thirdly, something is re-membering us, seeking its fullness through us. There is an archetypal field, an entelechy which moves us even at times when we are not aware or are uncooperative. Later, we often recognize that there was a purpose to our suffering, to what prized us out of the familiar and into the unknown. The psyche is objective; that is, it is not just our conscious experience of it, but something which wills us through history and experience. We speak of those organizational drives which develop us, protect us, lead us through danger, as instincts. Well, what are instincts?

An instinct is simply a word for the self-organizing and eschatological aspects of being. Psyche remembers us, whether we remember it or not. Even if we forget psyche, psyche does not forget us. It re-members through the building of blood and bone, the movements of soul. We are, indeed, carried by those great currents which embody history through each of us. Psyche re-members us backward and forward.

In re-membering psyche we affirm four of its qualities: mystery, autonomy, process and dialogue.

As we have seen, our philosophies, psychologies and theologies are "fictions," some of them useful. A fiction (from Latin *facere),* is not an untruth any more than myth is. It is a made thing, a construct. Fictions may serve us well, just as girders support traffic across a river. But as constructs they are also a form of untruth, a partiality which allows the larger truth to slip away, elude our grasp. The more I try to define psyche, the more it becomes an artifact of consciousness, and the more I lose relationship to it.

Psyche is autonomous; it wills itself whether we will or not. It is process. Ego seeks to reify, to hold, to fix, in service to anxiety management. But psyche overthrows this fantasy. The more we invest in a static concept of ourselves and our lives, the more likely we will suffer boredom or depression. Psyche will not be contained or fixed; it is dynamic, not static.

And lastly, it takes courage, strength, humility and constancy to dialogue with psyche. But if we do not do so, it will deal with us autonomously. In other words, when we do not observe, attend (which is what the word "therapy" means, from Greek *therapeuein)* psyche's presence in the symptomatology of everyday life, it will be pathologized and manifest as neurosis in the individual, and as conflict, hysteria, violence or mass possession at the group level.

Thus, the price we pay for not attending the healing of psyche is that terrible feeling of inauthentic suffering. The price we pay for pulling out of the ranks is guilt. Our redemption lies in bringing renewal, something unique, back to the group. We serve the group best, then, by being who we are, by discovering our uniqueness and sharing it with others.

The false self which we were obliged to assemble in the face of the demands of familial and cultural environments never feels quite right. Something is always trying to break through to us via intuitions, symptoms, dreams.

There is the story of a young rabbinical student who asked his teachers why God did not manifest in such grand ways today as he did to Moses and Abraham. Because, he is told, we do not stoop low enough to hear the voice of God. Usually we stoop low enough to hear psyche speak only when we have been knocked down and are forced to listen. It is a pleasant fantasy to think that that might not be necessary, but it doesn't happen that way. Put paid to another wishful thought.

Recall that the question of the first half of life is: "What does the world demand of me, and can I mobilize my resources in the face of fear and intimidation to meet those demands?" Just as surely, the question of the second half is: "What does the psyche (soul) ask of me?" A full life requires that we suffer and struggle with both questions.

Re-membering psyche is the task of homecoming. A number of years ago I found myself in a situation where someone asked where I lived. For a moment I dissociated, and a sort of internal monitor crawled slowly before my mind's eye. After a few awkward seconds I started to say, "Zurich," even though I lived in New Jersey at the time. Then, in another of those split seconds, I thought that such an answer would not be understood, so I replied, finally, with the name of the town in which I lived.

Later, as I mused on this peculiar experience, I realized that my psyche had told me something very important. Where we live is not necessarily where we physically live, but rather how we live in psyche's realm. "Zurich" for me was, and still is, a symbol of my humbling, developmental journey, and of the final acceptance that something larger than ego was running my life. No matter where I live, my journey is my home.

Whether I forget psyche or not, it will not forget me. It is no accident that the German word for "memory" is *Erinnerung*, literally the act of inner-ing. Re-membering psyche is the experience of being present to the constancy of the inner world, that which moves us from within, and which subsequently makes personal and cultural history in the outer world. This is homecoming, to be at home on the journey, where psyche is our constant companion amid ever-changing landscapes.

This theme of re-membering is hardly new. It has been the mindful task of many before us. One thinks of Plato, twenty-six centuries ago, in the *Meno:*

> One cannot seek for what he knows, and it seems equally impossible for him to seek for what he does not know. For what one knows he cannot seek, since he knows it: and what he does not know he cannot seek since he does not even know for what to seek.[95]

Or in the third century, St. Augustine:

> I seek a happy life. . . . But how do I seek it? Is it by remembrance, as though I had forgotten it . . . ? Did we not know it, we should not love it.[96]

And Augustine again:

> Behold, thou were within and without, and thus did I seek thee. I, unlovely, rushed heedlessly among the things of beauty Thou madst. Thou wert with me, but I was not with thee.[97]

In the seventeenth century, Pascal wrote: "Console thyself, thou wouldst not be seeking me hadst thou not already found me."[98] And in the nineteenth century the German poet Friedrich Hölderlin: "That which thou seekest is near, and already coming to meet thee."[99]

All acknowledged this re-membrance, re-sonance, re-sounding of the eternal in that part of ourselves which is also eternal.

Re-membering psyche asks four attitudes or practices of us.

---

[95] Cited by Stanley R. Hopper "On the Naming of the Gods in Hölderlin and Rilke," in Carl Michaelson, ed., *Christianity and the Existentialists,* p. 161.
[96] *Confessions,* X, xx, p. 29.
[97] Ibid., X, xxvii, p. 38.
[98] *Pensées,* p. 149.
[99] Cited in Martin Heidegger, *Existence and Being,* p. 285.

First, we are obliged to "read" the world around us with a spiritual eye. The gods, trivialized, disdained, forgotten, are nonetheless everywhere; their tracks are in the daily newspaper, in dreams and in our tortured history.

Second, we are summoned to do our private work of personal growth, and thereby help the world. As William Stafford wrote,

> . . . it is important that awake people be awake.
> Or a breaking line may discourage us back to sleep.
> The signals we give: yes, and no, or maybe should be clear.
> The darkness around us is deep.[100]

Thirdly, to recall that our life is not a place but a journey, not an answer but a question. Individuation is a process not a destination. We are not our history, although it is of us; we are the quality and temper of our journey.

And fourthly, we must come to bless this fragile life just as we find it, and be grateful for it. After all, it is the only life we have. No matter what the suffering, the senselessness and the angst, there is always the soul and the Self.

Compassion and Imagination

What matters? Perhaps only compassion and imagination. I believe that consciousness matters, but if push came to shove, I would put compassion first, imagination second, and consciousness third. Compassion (from Latin *passio)*, is the capacity to share the suffering of others, even as empathy and sympathy (from Greek *pathos)* imply the going out of our skin to visit the possibility of the other's experience.

Buddhism offers a great contribution by focusing on the fact that our common condition is suffering, a suffering which is only increased by the ego's desire to control or contain it. We are told that the threatening twin figures that grace the entry of many Buddhist temples represent fear and desire, and that one

---

[100] "A Ritual To Read to Each Other," in *The Darkness Around Us Is Deep: Selected Poems of William Stafford*, pp. 135f.

may enter the temple only by going through them without being intimidated. Few of us are up to that task, any more than we are capable of loving our neighbors as Jesus counseled or keeping the Ten Commandments without tongue in cheek.

What grips each of us, and holds hostage such communities as Ireland and the Holy Lands in a cyclic grip of violence, is possession by the fear of otherness, which is then projected onto those on the other side. For example, the first sign of anxiety about one's sexuality is the denigration of someone else's. Why so much energy is spent on homophobia is the subject of another book, but we may be sure that the source is fear of the other—which as it happens we carry within ourselves—an otherness which may only be faced with candor and with personal integrity. D.H. Lawrence's short story "The Prussian Officer" is a good example of this.

In short, we seek most to repress what we cannot face within ourselves, hence the importance of knowing our shadow.

At the same time, once we come to know another person, or another culture, we are prone to identify with him, her or it and find our aggressive impulses untenable. Dehumanizing the enemy, as we know, is the chief goal of propaganda in wartime. But what we suffer from even more is a failure of imagination. The more poverty stricken our imagination, the more susceptible we are to propaganda, be it political, commercial or evangelical.

Almost two hundred years ago the poet Percy Bysshe Shelley suggested that the secret of morality was to be found not in our brain, but in our organ of imagination.[101] The more stunted it is, the less capable we are of transcending the limits of personal experience. In his defense of the value of poetry in particular and the arts in general, Shelley argued that the great secret of morality is the power of the imagination, a power which is enhanced by the arts.

Surely Shelley is correct. What one sees in the polarization of

---

[101] See "A Defense of Poetry," in *Critical Theory Since Plato*.

human societies is not only the shriek of unaddressed fear, but also the whimper of limited imaginations. The more impaired the ego, as in the more serious disorders, the more difficult the confrontation with fear. A man beats his spouse because he cannot imagine her to be different from his abusive mother. A woman remains with an abusive spouse because she cannot imagine a partner unlike her abusive father. Each is controlled by fear; each suffers from a lack of imagination.

On the other hand, as one woman said to me this very day, "I wish we could revitalize that old word 'resurrection.' It is too encrusted with churchly baggage, but in my A.A. group I see resurrection every day." This from a woman who has not only been able to face her fear, but has risked the re-imagination of the world around her. The ancient archetypal motif of resurrection does in fact occur on a daily basis. One need only accept the possibility that fear will not always rule, and that the image of another possibility is a trustworthy guide. Until we can re-image our possibilities, we will remain locked within the old force-field presented by fate. The constriction of our imagination is our greatest tragedy and the source of our deepest self-wounding.

In the end, we are only tiny frightened animals, doing our best to survive amid other tiny frightened animals. That we are fearful is inescapable, and that we lash out is all too clear, as the violent history of the world shows. But we also have a soul, and within the soul is the power to imagine the possibility of breaking the old mold and experiencing alternatives. Without compassion and imagination, our lives remain forever constrained within the small and the broken.

Risking compassion and imagining alternatives enlarges and deepens; it heals, always. How important it is to transcend our limits, to see the suffering of those who have hurt us, to see the *logos* behind their behaviors, to feel their suffering in the context of their limits. Like the Bodhisattvas of Buddhist tradition, one remains behind to succor, out of compassion. In Yeats's play *The Countess Kathleen*, the heroine refuses salvation as long as suffering in others continues.

Speaking of Kierkegaard's struggle with the limits of our condition, the theologian Paul Ricoeur observes:

> [Kierkegaard's] *The Concept of Dread* evokes the two ways in which a man may lose himself: in the infinite without finiteness or in the finite without infinity, in reality without possibility or in imagination without the efficacy of work, marriage, profession, political activity.[102]

Kierkegaard recognized that to be mired in the daily grind without the imaginal possibility of infinity is to be trapped; to drift in the clouds of floating possibilities without specific commitment is to have no effect. Thus, compassion binds us with eros to this world, which is our home, and imagination creates a larger world, which is our destiny.

The twin saving values of compassion and imagination come together in a poem by Linda McCarriston. She rides at night with her horse; she observes the world and is observed, concluding:

> The horse bears me along, like grace,
>
> making me better than I am,
> and what I think or say or see
> is whole in these moments, is neither
> small nor broken. For up, out of
> the inscrutable earth, have come my body
> and the separate body of the mare;
> flawed and aching and wronged. Who then
> is better made to say "be well, be glad,"
>
> or who to long that we, as one
> might course over the entire valley,
> over all valleys, as a bird in a great embrace
> of flight, who presses against her breast,
> in grief and tenderness,
> the whole weeping body of the world?[103]

---

[102] "The Reaffirmation of the Tragic," in H. Bloom, ed., *The Book of Job,* p. 8.
[103] "Riding Out at Evening," in *Talking Soft Dutch,* p. 71.

Living the Questions

If you began this book of questions looking for answers, I expect you are thoroughly frustrated by now. If I had answers I would not withhold them, but the truth is that there are no answers valid for all or for always. What is concluded today is superseded tomorrow, or reframed by the enlargement of the dilemma to include quite different values. Those different values provide the dialectic of growth and serve nature's purpose. Thus, the depression we had back then, the conflict that yesterday seemed intractable, became the catalyst for growth, for the next stage of the journey. Only later can one acknowledge the presence of forces of renewal at work, only later discern their secret service in the dark night of the soul. Thus, we cannot wait upon, or expect, answers, for whatever answers appear today we may outgrow tomorrow, only to be confronted with new questions.

Incredibly, we may finally conclude that the answers we once so desperately sought are not even very important. But the questions are, and they do not go away. When we risk living them in the days ahead, they will lead us to authenticity, and possibly to some useful understanding unique to our own moment.

The younger we are, the more frustrated we will be by this absence of clarity. The older we are, the more likely we can abide ambiguity. The more mature we are, the more we are able to tolerate not only ambiguity, but also the anxiety it may beget. In the end we realize that our journey is our home, and the quality of that home is a function of the questions we ask. If our prevailing question is how to find security or acceptance, or how to avoid this journey, we will remain forever the lost children of our lost, frightened parents, drifting through our inner deserts.

If our questions lead us to other and more complex questions, we will find a deeper life, richer, more rewarding, more interesting and, most astonishingly, our own intended life, not someone else's. In the end it is never about answers, which are always provisional and transitory. Rather it is about facing the challenge of the questions themselves. As Peter Matthiessen concludes:

> The secret of the mountains is that the mountains simply exist, as I
> do myself: the mountains exist simply, which I do not. The moun-
> tains have no "meaning," they *are* meaning; the mountains *are*.
> The sun is round. I ring with life, and the mountains ring, and when
> I can hear it, there is a ringing that we share. I understand all this,
> not in my mind but in my heart.[104]

When I was young, this would not have been good enough. Today it is so rich that I can hardly bear it.

After he has climbed every mountain and suffered great priva-
tion to see a snow leopard, and yet has failed to see one, Matthiessen is asked, "Have you seen the snow leopard?" "No," he replies, "Isn't that wonderful?"[105] This is the miraculous Zen-like
report of a man who has discovered that the snow leopard is not
the goal, but a metaphor for the journey.

What if we were to find the leopard of our dreams—happiness, God, the perfect partner, whatever? Could we bear it, first
of all, and then, could we stay there? Like Odysseus, would we
not have to wander in search of some still more distant shore?
The eighteenth-century theologian Gotthold Lessing said that
when we stand before the two hands of God—one holding the
truth, one the search for truth—that we should take the latter in
honor of the former.

In not seizing upon the hand holding a packaged truth, we
may experience guilt and anxiety. But it is just these perturba-
tions of the soul that keep us in a religious, which is to say, psychologically honest, position. Like the old Buddhist *koan*—if
you meet the Buddha on the road, kill him—we are most open to
the radical mystery precisely when we resist codifying it as an
artifact of ego consciousness and, most of all, when we have to
get back on the road in pursuit of its paradoxical permutations.

Recalling both that our lives begin with a traumatic separation

---

[104] *The Snow Leopard,* p. 212.
[105] Ibid., p. 246.

from the umbilical home and that the cradle of tribal mythos has faded like last autumn's leaves, we are left with the inescapable conclusion that the journey itself is our only home and our only hope for renewal.

Hemingway once said that if the story does not end in death, the story is not finished; so, though Homer brings Odysseus home, the *Odyssey* ends prematurely. The Greek poet Constantine Cavafy wondered what Odysseus would have experienced if he had really arrived home. In "Ithaca," he asks that Odysseus reflect awhile on the journey toward Ithaca and consider what it really means. He suggests to that fabled voyager on the wine-dark sea that Ithaca's service to him is not as eschatological goal, but as compelling motive for the journey itself. Why does the bear go over the mountain? Answer: to see what he can see. That is why. That is why we all go.

It is the journey *qua* journey that marks Odysseus as the archetypal wanderer, not his sitting comfortably in front of the telly quaffing a beer while watching the Athenians play the Spartans. It is the *idea* of Ithaca, the haunting imago of connection, which has brought him his rich, painful, interesting life.

> Ithaca has given you the beautiful voyage.
> Without her you would never have taken the road.
> But she has nothing more to give you.
> And if you find her poor, Ithaca has not defrauded you.
> With the great wisdom you have gained, with so much experience
> You must surely have understood by then what Ithacas mean.[106]

Living the questions, perhaps even learning to love them, keeps our life open-ended and therefore developing: they channel debilitating fear and vagrant desire into the progressive, differentiated distribution of energy; and most of all, they make our life more interesting to ourselves and others. If we embrace what our Ithacas mean, then we are living in a respectful relationship

---

[106] *The Complete Poems of Cavafy*, pp. 36f.

with the great mystery that courses through us, rather than seeking to reify and limit its potential.

This is no small matter. It is intimidating, but it brings the great, multifoliate cosmos to blossom through us—its singular, humble, wonderfully peculiar representatives. Recall Jung's remark: "Ultimately every individual life is at the same time the eternal life of the species."[107] And, as Rilke reminds us, "Oh, whoever's heart might learn to blossom, then / Might transcend the lesser dangers, and risk the Greatest."[108]

What is that danger? That we might learn to blossom *here, now . . .* we the most transient, blossoming here, *now.*

If the Self is experienced as a verb, as the psyche selving through us, then we are all servants to some larger force whose purpose is obscure though its intentions were once available to us as children. Given the dependency of childhood, we all suffered interference with our relationship to that intentionality. Perhaps this is what our ancestors collectively called the Fall, or what they called sin (actually an archery term, meaning "to miss the target's center"). But the recovery of our relationship to the Self's intention is surely what we call healing.

Our spiritual/psychological condition will never be cured, but it may be healed. Just as pain is physical, suffering is spiritual. Accordingly, we all experience the limits of our condition as a source of pain, but nonetheless must still wrestle with the Angel of Suffering to receive its blessing. Though it pull our bone from its socket, as with Jacob, we must not let go of the Angel of Suffering until it blesses us.

Stanley Kunitz wrote poetry into his nineties. "The Layers" seems to summarize what this whole book has been about. It is a metaphor for his progressively deepening experience of the levels of his journey. His personal report reminds the ego of its proclivity toward superficiality and invites transcendence of its

---

[107] "Psychology and Religion," *Psychology and Religion,* CW 11, par. 146.
[108] "The Almond Trees," in *Sämtliche Werke,* (Author's translation).

fear through a life-long encounter with fractured depths and frangible possibilities. Kunitz writes,

> I have wandered through many lives,
> some of them my own;
> and I am not who I was.
> Though some principle of being
> abides, from which I struggle
> not to stray.[109]

He goes on to record and lament, or celebrate, the friends and his own provisional identities lost along the way. Gladly would he abide, rest awhile, then go back to the old familiar places; gladly live on the surface of things amid "the litter;" gladly go shopping; gladly get stoned; gladly get laid; gladly chill out. But he cannot, will not.

> Yet I turn, I turn,
> exulting somewhat,
> with my will intact to go
> wherever I need to go . . . .
> In my darkest night . . .
> a nimbus-clouded voice
> directed me:
> "Live in the layers,
> not on the litter."
> Though I lack the art
> to decipher it,
> no doubt the next chapter
> in my book of transformations
> is already written.
> I am not done with my changes.

We too are not done with our changes.

Troubling questions summon us to a larger life. In the meantime we walk, we all walk, in shoes too small. On this journey we call our life, we are best served not by the answers which are but

---

[109] In *Passing Through: The Later Poems, New and Selected,* p. 108.

a seductive interregnum at best, but by questions which trouble us into growth. With conscientious struggle we may attain a larger life out of that trouble, and a death worthy of that life. Along the way we may also attain some love, some understanding, a lot of compassion, and, if we are lucky, a lot of trouble.

While the ultimate purpose of this journey and our unique role in the great scheme of things will remain a mystery, our questions serve us by keeping us on track. Something wants to live through us, and we need to allow it. Whence, and whither, this journey, is the question of questions. But then, we are familiar now with questions, for our life itself is a question. Again, as Jung so wisely put it,

> The meaning of my existence is that life has addressed a question to me . . . or conversely, I myself am a question.[110]

---

[110] *Memories, Dreams, Reflections*, p. 318.

Bibliography

Agee, James. *A Death in the Family*. New York: Bantam, 1957.

Auden, W.H. *Collected Poems*. New York: Random House, 1976.

Augustine, St. *Confessions*. London: Liveright, 1927.

Bloom, Harold, ed. *The Book of Job*. Philadelphia: Chelsea House Publishers, 1998.

Bly, Robert; Hillman, James; Meade, Michael, eds. *The Rag and Bone Shop of the Heart: Poems for Men*. New York: HarperCollins, 1992.

Bonhoeffer, Dietrich. *The Cost of Discipleship*. Chicago: Simon and Schuster, 1976.

Cavafy, C.P. "Ithaca." In *The Complete Poems of Cavafy*, Trans. Rae Dalven. New York: Harcourt, Brace and World, 1961.

Conrad, Joseph. *Heart of Darkness*. New York: W.W. Norton and Co., 1963.

Dunn, Stephen. *Different Hours*. New York: W.W. Norton and Co., 2000.

Edinger, Edward F. *Encounter with the Self: A Jungian Commentary on William Blake's* Illustrations of the Book of Job. Toronto: Inner City Books, 1986.

Eliot, T.S. *The Complete Poems and Plays: 1909-1950*. New York: Harcourt, Brace and World, 1952.

Ellmann, Richard, and O'Clair, Robert, eds. *Modern Poems: An Introduction to Poetry*. New York: W.W. Norton, Inc., 1973.

Foster, Thomas E., and Guthrie, Elizabeth C., eds. *A Year in Poetry*. New York: Random House, 1995.

Frey-Rohn, Liliane. "Evil from a Psychological Point of View." In *Spring 1965*.

Gordon, Lyndall. *T.S. Eliot: An Imperfect Life*: New York: W.W. Norton and Co., 2000.

Guthrie, W.K.C. *A History of Greek Philosophy,* vol. 1. Cambridge: Cambridge University Press, 1982.

Heidegger, Martin. *Being and Time.* San Francisco: HarperCollins, 1962.

_____. *Existence and Being.* New York: Vision Press, 1949.

Hollis, James. *The Eden Project: In Search of the Magical Other.* Toronto: Inner City Books, 1998.

_____. *The Middle Passage: From Misery to Meaning in Midlife.* Toronto: Inner City Books, 1993.

_____. *Swamplands of the Soul: New Life in Dismal Places.* Toronto: Inner City Books, 1996.

_____. *Tracking the Gods: The Place of Myth in Modern Life.* Toronto: Inner City Books, 1995.

Hopkins, Gerard Manley. *A Hopkins Reader.* Ed. John Pick. Garden City, N.Y.: Doubleday, 1966.

Hunter, J. Paul, ed. *The Norton Introducton to Poetry.* New York: W.W. Norton and Co., 1991.

Jung, C.G. *The Collected Works* (Bollingen Series XX). 20 vols. Trans. R.F.C. Hull, Ed. H. Read, M. Fordham, G. Adler, Wm. McGuire. Princeton: Princeton University Press, 1953-1979.

_____. *Letters* (Bollingen Series XCV). 2 vols. Ed. Gerhard Adler and Aniela Jaffé. Princeton: Princeton University Press, 1973.

_____. *Memories, Dreams, Reflections.* Trans. Richard and Clara Winston. Ed. Aniela Jaffe. New York: Vintage Books, 1965.

Kazantzakis, Nikos. *The Last Temptation of Christ.* New York: Simon and Schuster, 1960.

Kierkegaard, Soren. *Papers and Journals: A Selection.* Trans. Alastar Hannay, London: Penguin Books, 1996.

Kübler-Ross, Elizabeth. *Living with Death and Dying.* New York: MacMillan, 1951.

Kunitz, Stanley. *Passing Through: The Later Poems, New and Selected.* New York: W.W. Norton and Co., 1995.

Lawrence, D.H. "The Prussian Officer." In *The Prussian Officer and Other Stories.* Oxford: Oxford University Press, 1995.

Matthiessen, Peter. *The Snow Leopard.* New York: Penguin Books, 1987.

MacLeish, Archibald. *J.B.* Boston: Houghton-Mifflin, 1956.

McCarriston, Linda. *Talking Soft Dutch.* Lubbock, TX: Texas Technical University Press, 1984.

Michaelson, Carl, ed. *Christianity and the Existentialists.* New York: Charles Scribner's Sons, 1956.

Pascal, Blaise. *Pensées.* New York: Dutton and Co., 1958.

Pickstock, Catharine. *After Writing: On the Liturgical Consummation of Philosophy.* Oxford: Blackwell, 1998.

Recer, Paul. "Scientists Solve Firefly Mystery." *The Associated Press,* June 28, 2001.

Rilke, Rainer Maria. *The Duino Elegies.* New York: W.W. Norton, Inc., 1963.

_____. *Letters to a Young Poet.* Trans. M.D. Herter Norton. New York: W.W. Norton and Co., 1962.

_____. *Sämtliche Werke.* Frankfurt am Main: Insel Verlag, 1955-66.

_____. *Sonnets to Orpheus.* New York: W.W. Norton Inc., 1962.

Sharp, Daryl. *Chicken Little: The Inside Story.* Toronto: Inner City Books, 1993.

Shelley, Percy Bysshe. *Critical Theory Since Plato.* Ed. Hazard Adams. New York: Harcourt, Brace, Jovanovich, 1970.

Shipley, Joseph T. *Dictionary of Word Origins.* Totowa, NJ: Littlefield, Adams and Co., 1967.

Stafford, William. *The Darkness Around Us Is Deep: Selected Poems of William Stafford.* Ed. Robert Bly. New York: Harper, 1993.

Thomas, Dylan. *Collected Poems.* New York: New Directions Publishing Co., 1946.

Tolstoy, Leo. "The Death of Ivan Ilyich." In *The Death of Ivan Ilyich and Other Stories.* New York: New American Library, 1960.

Yeats, W.B. *The Countess Kathleen.* In *The Collected Plays of W.B. Yeats.* New York: Macmillan, 1965.

_____. *Selected Poems and Two Plays.* Ed. M.L. Rosenthal. New York: MacMillan, 1962.

Index

Also by James Hollis in this Series

THE MIDDLE PASSAGE: From Misery to Meaning in Midlife
ISBN 0-919123-60-0. (1993) 128pp. *Sewn* $16
Why do so many go through so much disruption in their middle years? Why then? What does it mean and how can we survive it? Hollis shows how we can pass through midlife consciously, rendering the second half of life all the richer and more meaningful.

UNDER SATURN'S SHADOW
The Wonding and Healing of Men
ISBN 0-919123-64-3. (1994) 144pp. *Sewn* $16
Saturn was the Roman god who ate his children to stop them from usurping his power. Men have been psychologically and spiritually wounded by this legacy. Hollis offers a new perspective on the secrets men carry in their hearts, and how they may be healed.

TRACKING THE GODS: The Place of Myth in Modern Life
ISBN 0-919123-69-4. (1995) 160pp. *Sewn* $16
Whatever our religious background or personal psychology, a greater intimacy with myth provides a vital link with meaning, the absence of which is so often behind the neuroses of our time. Here Hollis explains why a connection with our mythic roots is crucial for us as individuals and as responsible citizens.

SWAMPLANDS OF THE SOUL: New Life in Dismal Places
ISBN 0-919123-74-0. (1996) 160pp. *Sewn* $16
Who does not long to arrive some distant day at that sunlit meadow where we may live in pure contentment? Yet much of the time we are lost in the quicksands of guilt, anxiety, betrayal, grief, doubt, loss, loneliness, despair, anger, obsessions, addictions, depression and the like. Perhaps the goal of life is not happiness but meaning.

THE EDEN PROJECT
In Search of the Magical Other
ISBN 0-919123-80-5. (1998) 160pp. *Sewn* $16
A timely and thought-provoking corrective to the fantasies about relationships that permeate Western culture. Here is a challenge to greater personal responsibility—a call for individual growth as opposed to seeking rescue from others.

CREATING A LIFE: Finding Your Individual Path
ISBN 0-919123-93-7. (2001) 160pp. *Sewn* $16
With insight and compassion grounded in the humanist side of analytical psychology, Hollis elucidates the circuitous path of individuation. A powerful commentary on the importance of the examined life, illustrating how we may come to an understanding of our life choices and relationships by exploring our core complexes and personal history.

Studies in Jungian Psychology
by Jungian Analysts

Quality Paperbacks

Prices and payment in $US (except in Canada, $Cdn)

The Secret Raven: Conflict and Transformation
Daryl Sharp (Toronto). ISBN 0-919123-00-7. 128 pp. $16

The Psychological Meaning of Redemption Motifs in Fairy Tales
Marie-Louise von Franz (Zürich). ISBN 0-919123-01-5. 128 pp. $16

Alchemy: An Introduction to the Symbolism and the Psychology
Marie-Louise von Franz (Zürich). ISBN 0-919123-04-X. 288 pp. $20

Descent to the Goddess: A Way of Initiation for Women
Sylvia Brinton Perera (New York). ISBN 0-919123-05-8. 112 pp. $16

Addiction to Perfection: The Still Unravished Bride
Marion Woodman (Toronto). ISBN 0-919123-11-2. 208 pp. $18pb/$25hc

Jungian Dream Interpretation: A Handbook of Theory and Practice
James A. Hall, M.D. (Dallas). ISBN 0-919123-12-0. 128 pp. $16

The Creation of Consciousness: Jung's Myth for Modern Man
Edward F. Edinger (Los Angeles). ISBN 0-919123-13-9. 128 pp. $16

The Analytic Encounter: Transference and Human Relationship
Mario Jacoby (Zürich). ISBN 0-919123-14-7. 128 pp. $16

Change of Life: Dreams and the Menopause
Ann Mankowitz (Ireland). ISBN 0-919123-15-5. 128 pp. $16

The Illness That We Are: A Jungian Critique of Christianity
John P. Dourley (Ottawa). ISBN 0-919123-16-3. 128 pp. $16

Cultural Attitudes in Psychological Perspective
Joseph L. Henderson, M.D. (San Francisco). ISBN 0-919123-18-X. 128 pp. $16

The Vertical Labyrinth: Individuation in Jungian Psychology
Aldo Carotenuto (Rome). ISBN 0-919123-19-8. 144 pp. $16

The Pregnant Virgin: A Process of Psychological Transformation
Marion Woodman (Toronto). ISBN 0-919123-20-1. 208 pp. $18pb/$25hc

Encounter with the Self: William Blake's *Illustrations of the Book of Job*
Edward F. Edinger (Los Angeles). ISBN 0-919123-21-X. 80 pp. $15

The Scapegoat Complex: Toward a Mythology of Shadow and Guilt
Sylvia Brinton Perera (New York). ISBN 0-919123-22-8. 128 pp. $16

The Jungian Experience: Analysis and Individuation
James A. Hall, M.D. (Dallas). ISBN 0-919123-25-2. 176 pp. $18

Phallos: Sacred Image of the Masculine
Eugene Monick (Scranton, PA). ISBN 0-919123-26-0. 144 pp. $16

Touching: Body Therapy and Depth Psychology
Deldon Anne McNeely (Lynchburg, VA). ISBN 0-919123-29-5. 128 pp. $16

Personality Types: Jung's Model of Typology
Daryl Sharp (Toronto). ISBN 0-919123-30-9. 128 pp. $16

The Sacred Prostitute: Eternal Aspect of the Feminine
Nancy Qualls-Corbett (Birmingham). ISBN 0-919123-31-7. 176 pp. $18

When the Spirits Come Back
Janet O. Dallett (Seal Harbor, WA). ISBN 0-919123-32-5. 160 pp. $16

The Mother: Archetypal Image in Fairy Tales
Sibylle Birkhäuser-Oeri (Zürich). ISBN 0-919123-33-3. 176 pp. $18

The Survival Papers: Anatomy of a Midlife Crisis
Daryl Sharp (Toronto). ISBN 0-919123-34-1. 160 pp. $16

The Cassandra Complex: Living with Disbelief
Laurie Layton Schapira (New York). ISBN 0-919123-35-X. 160 pp. $16

Acrobats of the Gods: Dance and Transformation
Joan Dexter Blackmer (Wilmot Flat, NH). ISBN 0-919123-38-4. 128 pp. $16

Eros and Pathos: Shades of Love and Suffering
Aldo Carotenuto (Rome). ISBN 0-919123-39-2. 160 pp. $16

The Ravaged Bridegroom: Masculinity in Women
Marion Woodman (Toronto). ISBN 0-919123-42-2. 224 pp. $20

The Dream Story
Donald Broadribb (Baker's Hill, Australia). ISBN 0-919123-45-7. 256 pp. $20

The Rainbow Serpent: Bridge to Consciousness
Robert L. Gardner (Toronto). ISBN 0-919123-46-5. 128 pp. $16

Circle of Care: Clinical Issues in Jungian Therapy
Warren Steinberg (New York). ISBN 0-919123-47-3. 160 pp. $16

Jung Lexicon: A Primer of Terms & Concepts
Daryl Sharp (Toronto). ISBN 0-919123-48-1. 160 pp. $16

Body and Soul: The Other Side of Illness
Albert Kreinheder (Los Angeles). ISBN 0-919123-49-X. 112 pp. $16

The Secret Lore of Gardening: Patterns of Male Intimacy
Graham Jackson (Toronto). ISBN 0-919123-53-8. 160 pp. $16

Getting To Know You: The Inside Out of Relationship
Daryl Sharp (Toronto). ISBN 0-919123-56-2. 128 pp. $16

Conscious Femininity: Interviews with Marion Woodman
Introduction by Marion Woodman (Toronto). ISBN 0-919123-59-7. 160 pp. $16

Chicken Little: The Inside Story *(A Jungian Romance)*
Daryl Sharp (Toronto). ISBN 0-919123-62-7. 128 pp. $16

Coming To Age: The Croning Years and Late-Life Transformation
Jane R. Prétat (Providence, RI). ISBN 0-919123-63-5. 144 pp. $16

Digesting Jung: Food for the Journey
Daryl Sharp (Toronto). ISBN 0-919123-96-1. 128 pp. $16

The Cat: A Tale of Feminine Redemption
Marie-Louise von Franz (Zurich). ISBN 0-919123-84-8. 128 pp. $16

Animal Guides: In Life, Myth and Dreams
Neil Russack (San Francisco). ISBN 0-919123-98-8. 224 pp. $20

Discounts: any 3-5 books, 10%; 6-9 books, 20%; 10 or more, 25%

Add Postage (surface): 1-2 books, $3; 3-4 books, $5; 5-9 books, $10; 10 or more, free

Write or phone for free Catalogue of **over 100 titles** and **Jung at Heart** newsletter

INNER CITY BOOKS, Box 1271, Station Q, Toronto, ON M4T 2P4, Canada
Tel. 416- 927-0355   /   Fax 416-924-1814   /   E-mail info@innercitybooks.net